Miss Di Tells Her Stories

by

Diana Gabhart

Dr. Herbert Gabhart
204 Longwood Court
Nashville, TN 37215
(615) 269-5381

Book design: JM Productions, Brentwood, Tennessee
Cover design: Ron Watson

Printed in the United States of America

Dedication

This book carries a threefold dedication.

It is dedicated to the hundreds of children and youth who sat at Miss Di's feet either in the classroom or in the morning worship service or wherever else she served. They provided Diana the opportunity to which she gave her best trying to inspire and lead them onward in Christian growth. This was her consuming passion. In this area, special dedication is made to her niece, Jennie Aleshire; and to her nephews, Jonathan Aleshire, Will Smith, and Matt Smith.

It is also dedicated to Helen and Ed Kennedy, longtime friends, whose generous support helped to make the publication of this book possible, and to Dottie Aiken, a close friend for many years.

It is likewise dedicated to the staff and members of the First Baptist Church of Decatur, Georgia, who surrounded her with love, encouragement, and Christian fellowship, and to her host of friends, far and near.

Foreword

Diana Ruth Gabhart was my dearest friend until her untimely death in March, 1994. We shared much together as good friends do — even in our work. As a former Director of Children's Work in the Tennessee Church Training Department at the Tennessee Baptist Convention, I would share successful/proven ideas and projects that would work in the local church. Always in need in my own church for themes and ideas on Children's Day, Children's Retreats, plus other such emphases, she was the friend who either called or sent via overnight mail the information needed to meet my deadline. But, we never shared children's sermons since I was not the one who did this in my church. For a number of years I heard of Diana's children's sermon and her basket full of objects from both her children and congregation. Diana had the knowledge of not only being a teacher of the Bible, but also from fifteen years of public school teaching in Tennessee and Georgia. Many of her illustrations exemplify this gifted talent.

How grateful we are that Diana was willing for her children's sermons to be taped, and that First Baptist Church, Decatur, Georgia, preserved them. It is through this collection that we will all benefit and be blessed as we read her beautiful and meaningful illustrations which are woven with Bible stories and Scripture.

Use them. Tell them to your boys and girls with love. That is how Diana told them.

Helen Kennedy
(Mrs. Edward C. Kennedy)
Nashville, Tennessee

Introduction

Some people are gifted. Others are disciplined. Diana Gabhart was graced with both. She had a gift of love for children, the gift of understanding and insight. She could go inside a child's world. Her Christian devotion expressed itself naturally in an orderly discipline that eventuated in impactful outcomes. She planned exceptionally well, including her children's sermons.

Miss Gabhart came to our church staff from a high competence recognized by the local school system here in Decatur. Long before she was installed as minister of children in the church, she already had earned a community reputation as an award winning teacher of children in the Westchester Elementary School. She brought a maturity, a sense of excellence, along with a life-time love of the church when she accepted God's call to make a transition in her life's work. Diana began to grow in new ways in a calling that may have been underlying all along.

Diana chose her parents well. Dr. and Mrs. Gabhart provided such an exceptional launching pad from their thoroughly Christian family. Diana's wonderful values and commitment to Christian missions derived from that wonderful family source.

Having no children of her own, our church youth sought Diana out every Mother's Day to present her a flower. The youth nicknamed her "Lady Di." As her pastor, I had the privilege of knowing her heart. Her love of Sword Drills, Vacation Bible School, and discipleship classes told me about what she cared.

I can see it now. Before the congregation was fully nestled into their pews after the first hymn, she had already launched into her children's sermon. It was a trademark. She brought her basket filled with fascinating contents. Invariably, the children's attention riveted on the items and on her. Children were painlessly, age appropriately, learning to worship in "big church." There were unforgettable teachable moments. And they saw something of God in the face of Miss Gabhart.

Her presentations to the children were profoundly visual in nature. She did not so much tell canned stories, but rather engaged her children in a creative step at a time. She took them on a journey. She met them where they were. She did such interesting things with her objects from the magic basket. Inevitably she came to a very naturally chosen verse of scripture at the close and had the children bow their heads to pray. It was quite a moment in the sanctuary of the First Baptist Church for adults who had welcomed the opportunity to overhear the children's sermon. And children felt like worship enfolded them in a special way.

Within this book are models and examples of innovative ways to do sermons for children in today's church. They are also repeatable. You can fill your basket with similar items and engage your children in Christian education.

She sat in queenly fashion on the steps of the platform in the sanctuary. The children came from all parts of the church and found their way to the front. The children were wide-eyed sitting around her, eagerly waiting for the hymn to end and the story to start. She elicited response along the way. Sometimes the children broke out in laughter. Always their faces reflected their glowing understanding. They sometimes said amusing, unexpected things out loud! Diana nurtured them toward a faith experience with the living Christ! So can you.

Peter Rhea Jones, Pastor
First Baptist Church, Decatur, Georgia

Contents

Part II — Special Days 75

Part I

Scripture for Part I
(page numbers are in **boldface**)

Secret Agents and Sequoias

The oldest living things are the giant Sequoia trees. These trees can be as much as 300 feet tall. They were around before the birth of Jesus. In fact, some of them are as much as 4,000 years old! I brought this yardstick because the bark alone on these trees can be anywhere from one to three feet thick. So it's very resistant to fire damage or any insects that might try to damage it. These trees are found on the slopes of the Sierra Nevada Mountains in California.

Let's think about those trees. Think about a twenty-story building. Those trees can be as tall as that. The trunk of the tree is as big as the average size of someone's living room. I would have to flip this yardstick twenty-three times to show you how long one single branch is—70 feet. The Psalmist told us about something that is big and tall. "Your constant love reaches above the heavens. Your faithfulness touches the sky" (Psalm 36:5). That's God's love for us, but it's hard for us to imagine that His love can be that big and high. He loves us that much.

Why is it so hard for us, then, to share His love with other people and to tell about His love to our friends? Do you squirm sometimes at school if somebody is talking about the kids who go to church on Wednesdays or Sundays? Does that make you uneasy? Are you willing to stick up for Jesus in school? Are you willing to go up to the class president or the captain of the football team and say, "Hey, let me tell you about Jesus?"

In old movies they used to have a "secret agent." I'm sure you've seen this. They always wore a trench coat and had it belted around their waist. They put these hats on their heads and pulled them down over one eye. I think many of us are acting like "secret agent Christians." Look inside my raincoat. There's a cross on the inside, but when I put it on, what happens? I button it up, and I don't let other people know I'm a Christian. We care about what our friends think, but don't we care about what Jesus thinks? We can't always sit on the fence and say, "Oh, I'm going to be right here, and I don't have to let them know I'm a Christian." There will be times at school when you'll have to make a decision about whether to cheat, whether to turn your homework in, and how you're going to act. You'll need to act like Christians. Sometimes you'll have to take a chance because our God loves us. We don't want to sit there and do nothing. I don't mean I want you to go to school with a jacket on that has Bible verses all over it. I don't want you to corner your friends in the hall and start preaching to them. I don't say you have to carry a big Bible with you that weighs ten tons. But I think we can't sit there and do nothing if we truly love Jesus. His love is so big and high we ought to share it. Romans 1:16 says, "For I am not ashamed of the gospel. It is the power of God for salvation to everyone who believes."

Let's pray. *Dear Father, Your love is so big, it's hard for us to believe how much You really care for us. Help us not to be "secret-agent Christians," but to show Your love and to share it with our friends. In Jesus' name. Amen.*

OBJECTS: Trench Coat (raincoat)/Picture of Sequoia tree

Don't Be an Empty Can!

If I take these cans and shake them, you don't hear a lot of noise. I could hit them together, and you hear only a little bit of sound. Suppose I emptied the cans and tied a piece of string to them. Now what happens? Why did I get so much noise? Because they are empty and clanging together. One thing I want you to remember is just because they make a loud noise, they may not be the most valuable.

In the New Testament we read about Paul. Paul was probably one of the greatest letter writers of all time. As a great Christian, he would go around and visit different churches. When he would come back from visiting those churches, he would write them a letter. In the letter he might give them encouragement or advice, or he might even scold them a little for the faults they had.

In one of Paul's letters, 1 Corinthians, there is a favorite passage. It's called "The Love Chapter," and it is 1 Corinthians 13. I want to read you the very first verse of that chapter. "If I speak in the tongues of men and of angels, but have not love, I am a noisy gong or a clanging cymbal." What does that mean to us as preschoolers and children? Later on, Paul said that if you did all the good deeds in the whole world, but you didn't have love and goodwill in your heart, they are empty actions, just like these empty cans.

I'll give you another example. Suppose you read your Sunday School lesson, learn your Bible verse, come back the next Sunday, and you are so proud. You sit down at your table, say your Bible verse to your teacher, sit up real straight, and you're real sure everyone heard you. Don't get me wrong, I want you to learn your Bible verse. But, suppose you only learned your Bible verse, and you didn't really learn what it meant, and in not learning what it meant, you did not do goodwill to others. Then that verse says you become as what? A noisy gong, a clanging cymbal, or like my empty cans.

One more example. Suppose you help your mother and father all day. You do errands. They ask you to take out the garbage. You even straightened up your room a little bit. Maybe you divided your toys out into some you are going to keep and some you are going to give away. But in the back of your mind you kept thinking, Boy, I've been really good today. Maybe I'll get to go to that movie tonight. If you have helped your parents all day and done it because you wanted something special to happen in return, and you did not have love and goodwill in your heart, then the Bible says you become as a noisy gong, a clanging cymbal, or like these empty cans, because this passage says, "Love is everything."

Let's pray. *Dear Father, may we do our good deeds everyday. May they be done in quietness and always in love. Amen.*

OBJECT: Tin Cans

God: The Greatest Counter

I need you to do some counting for me this morning. If I ask you to look up in the choir and count how many people are up there, I know all of you could count them. If I ask you to count the number of people in the sanctuary, you could do it, but you would probably have to go up and down the aisles, wouldn't you? Do you remember when you first learned to count? You learned to count on your fingers. You went: 1, 2, 3. Do you remember how proud your mother and daddy were when they would say, "How old are you?" and you could hold up your fingers. They would say, "Wow, you sure are smart. You know how old you are."

A lot of the people we are going to honor today certainly can't count their birthdays on their fingers anymore, but some of you still can. We went from counting on our fingers to first grade. When we got in first grade, we had flash cards and started learning our facts. I remember drilling on those facts. We had tests on them until we finally learned how to add. We went to the third grade, and we had to learn to multiply. Some of you still know how to multiply by 9s on your fingers. That's a special trick. Some of you are still using your fingers, but you know we don't use our heads or our fingers much when we add or multiply.

What are some other things we use? Adding machines. Calculators. Some of you even use computers, don't you? You feed all those numbers in, and those machines take care of everything. It's almost to the point we don't even know how to add or multiply anymore on our own. They have memory buttons, and we punch everything into them. But there's one person who can add and remember everything better than any machine. That person is God. He counts each one of you. He knows you by name. He knows where you live. He knows what you like to do. He never forgets.

We find a story in Luke 12 where Jesus was speaking to a crowd of people. They just kept coming in—a lot of them. The Bible even

88888888888888888

says they stepped on each other's toes. Jesus decided to use this as a lesson to those people, and this is what the Bible says. "In the meantime, when so many thousands of the multitude had gathered together that they trod upon one another, He began to say to His disciples first, are not five sparrows sold for two pennies, and not one of them is ever forgotten by God. Why, even the hairs of your head are numbered." God's counting always keeps up with each one of us. He never forgets us. He continues to count and take care of us.

Let's pray. *Dear Father, we're glad that You can count better than any calculator or computer because we know that You keep up with us. You never forget us, and we thank You for it. In Jesus' name. Amen.*

OBJECTS: Adding Machine/Calculator

Things a Credit Card Can't Buy

Have you ever thought about running away from home? Have you ever had a bad fight with your parents where they maybe said you couldn't do something you wanted to do, and you momentarily thought you just might pack up and run away? You wanted to get out of the house the best and fastest way you could. Maybe you simply thought about packing a lunch: sandwich, chips, and a Coke. Perhaps you thought about taking your favorite stuffed animal, but that's about all you thought of.

I remember my mother telling me of the time she and her brother decided to run away from home. They packed their bags and started down the sidewalk. They got to the first intersection, stopped because their mother told them never to cross the street, and went back home. Many times in old movies or television you've seen a hobo. We don't have so-called hobos, but you've seen pictures of them, and you know that they supposedly carried all of their belongings in a bandanna on a stick, hopped rides on old railroads, and travelled up and down the country.

I read a story one time about a rich man whose son really was going to leave home. The rich man tried every way he could to get his son not to leave home. His son said, "No. I've just got to do it. I don't like it here. I want to leave." The father said, "Well, let me give you a small gift. It's something very, very tiny. As long as you have this small gift with you, you will never be hungry, you'll always have clothes to wear, you can always stop at a motel and take a shower, and you can always ride a plane." So he gave him this very small gift. It's probably not what you thought. What was it? A credit card. Because this father, this earthly father figured that as long as he paid the bills on this credit card, his son would have everything he needed.

We know there are things a credit card cannot buy. It can't buy us love, buy us joy, buy us happiness or comfort. It certainly can't buy us eternal life with Jesus! Our Heavenly Father has promised us that we will have those things. I want to read a promise to you, and I've called it the Philippians 4:19 charge card, "And my God will supply every need of your according to His riches in glory in Christ Jesus."

Let's pray. *Dear Father, thank You for this promise, the promise of supplying our needs: love, joy, comfort, eternal life. Amen.*

OBJECTS: Bandanna/Credit Card

Playdough in God's Hands

What do I have? Playdough. I know all of you at one time or another have used Playdough. It's very soft and pliable. You can take it in your hands and make all sorts of things out of it. Some of you take that Playdough, twist it around, roll it, and you finally wind up with some kind of snake or lizard. Or, I could take that same roll, pinch it around, and I might have something that looks like a doughnut. We could pretend, couldn't we? The Bible says we are like Playdough in God's hands. Isaiah 64:8 says, "...We are the clay, and You our potter. And all we are the work of your hand." So what God is trying to do is take that clay and help mold us into something very beautiful. We become that way when we study His Word and listen to what it says, when we try to be the kind of Christian He wants us to be, and when we pray to Him.

What happens to this Playdough if I leave it out of the can? It dries out and gets very hard. That's what can happen to our lives if we don't let God continue to take that Playdough and help us mold our lives. There is a different kind of clay called Mexican clay, which many of you have used at school. You put it in a kiln and what you have made becomes very hard. Here are a little giraffe and a little bird that some children made for me. But you know what? They will always be like this. They are hard, and they will never change, will they? I have some statues made out of another type of clay. They are very beautiful to me. I put them on a shelf and look at them. They won't ever change unless I drop them and break them into a million pieces. They are hard and already what they are going to be.

The greatest thrill to those of us here at church who see you on Sunday mornings and on Wednesday nights is to know what God makes of you as He takes that clay and helps to shape your lives. As we see the sparkle in your eyes, the smiles, as we listen to what you are learning week by week, as we watch you grow as Christians, and see what you are letting God help you to become, that beautiful girl, that handsome boy, that very special person you are.

For our prayer today, I want to use the words of a song we sing here at church. So as we bow our heads I want you to listen to the words. *Have Thine own way, Lord. Have Thine own way. Thou art the potter. I am the clay. Mold me and make me after Thy will. While I am waiting, yielded and still. Amen.*

OBJECT: Playdough

Bring Fun With You?

See this medicine bag I have? You know that it's a medicine bag because it has a red heart on it like the Red Cross. In it I put something that some people say is the very best medicine in the world. You want to look in and see what it is? (recorded laughter) I hope that is the only twenty seconds of that you hear this time.

Some people say that laughter is the best medicine in the world. You know how it makes you feel when you laugh. A lot of you started laughing, and you feel happy and good when you hear that, don't you? God wants us to be happy and laugh. Do you know that we are the only creature He made who can laugh? We are the only ones! Somebody is going to say, "Wait a minute! That's not right. There is an animal who can laugh—the laughing hyena." But that's not true. Scientists have studied the laughing hyena, and they found out he not laughing: he is burping!

If I were going to take this basket with me on a trip to Stone Mountain for a picnic, I'd like to put a lot of good things in it. I would put fried chicken, sandwiches, potato chips, deviled eggs, carrots, and celery. I'd put a blanket to sit on and maybe a tablecloth, but once I got to Stone Mountain, I'd hope that everything I'd need for my picnic would be in here, because I couldn't walk in the back door and get anything else. Could I?

But we sometimes forget to take our good times with us. You may say, "What does she mean about good times?" Once I heard a little boy at a picnic come up to his father and say, "I'm having a terrible time. Let's go home." I waited to see what the father was going to say. The father thought and thought, and guess what? He didn't stop talking to his friends. He didn't get up and go play with his son, and he didn't give him a dollar and tell him to go buy himself some ice cream or a balloon. The father looked at his son and said, "Maybe you forgot to bring your fun with you. Did you think about that?" The little boy sort of looked at his father, and then he started smiling. He said, "I can find somebody to play ball with me, and you know what would be even more fun? If we went under those bushes over there and told ghost stories.''

Carry your good times with you. Carry happy thoughts with you. God wants us to rejoice, and He often told people to rejoice. In Psalm 67:4 we find this verse, ''Come, let us sing for joy to the Lord.'' There are many, many Bible verses about being joyful and happy, but I want to close with this one from Nehemiah 8:10, ''For this day is holy and to our Lord. For the joy of our Lord is your strength.''

Let us pray. *Father, we are thankful today that we have joy in our hearts. We are thankful that we can sing praises and rejoice in Your name. You have given us such a beautiful world to make us happy. Amen.*

OBJECTS: Medicine Bag/Recorded Laughter

Living Proof

I have a sign in my hand. Can you read it? It says, ''I doubt it.'' A lot of people were late getting to Sunday School this morning because they forgot to set their clocks ahead. Suppose your Sunday School teacher had come in this morning and said, ''Oh, I'm so sorry I'm late, but a circus truck overturned in my yard, and tigers, lions, and monkeys were all over my yard''? You probably would've put your hands on your hips and said, ''I doubt it,'' wouldn't you?

This is a magnifying glass. If you hold it up, it makes the words bigger and makes the picture so you can see it better, but it also does something else. If I were to hold this glass where the sun touched it for a long time, a fire could start underneath it. What if I told you that a crow set a church on fire? You know what you'd tell me? ''I doubt it.'' But it really happened in North Carolina in a church about twenty years ago. They found a crow's nest up in the bell tower, and you know what was in the crow's nest? One of these magnifying glasses. Somehow the crow had gotten it up there, and a fire had started.

Jesus had a disciple who used this phrase, "I doubt it." Jesus rose from the tomb. He came back to visit His disciples. Everybody was in the room except for Thomas. Thomas wasn't there, so the other disciples said, "Thomas, we've seen Jesus. He's alive; He's back with us." You know what Thomas said? "I doubt it." He wanted some proof, didn't he?

When someone goes fishing, and they tell you they caught a fish this big, you want to see the fish, don't you? Or, if someone is in a race, and they tell you they won first place, you want to see that blue ribbon, don't you? Thomas wanted proof. Thomas said, "I will believe if I can see in His hand the prints of the nails and put my fingers into the prints of the nails." Then Thomas would believe. Well, eight days later all of the disciples were in a room together - all twelve of them. Thomas was there, and the door was locked. All of a sudden Thomas saw Jesus standing beside him. Jesus said, "Thomas, peace be unto you. Come up here and feel My hands and feel the nail prints." Thomas saw Jesus there, and he no longer doubted, did he? He didn't say he doubted then, because he saw Jesus. He bowed down to Jesus and said, "My Lord and my master." He now believed that Jesus had come back (see John 20).

Let's pray. *Father, we are thankful that Thomas was able to see Jesus and to believe, but we are so thankful that we don't have to see Jesus to believe. Amen.*

OBJECTS: Sign—I Doubt It / Magnifying Glass

Honor Your Parents

Today I want to talk to you about parents. If you wake up in the middle of the night, who do you wake up if you have had a bad dream? Probably your mother and father. Who would you go to if you needed some help with your homework? Maybe your dad or your mom. Parents are there to help us, aren't they? Did you know that the first word you ever learned to say (when you go home ask your parents or when you return to your seats) was either "da-da" or "ma-ma." Your parents were taking care of you, and those were the words you learned to speak first. Parents and children make up a family, and a family is a home.

There's a story about a little girl who was five years old. She moved to Japan, and her family was having trouble finding a place to live. They were staying in a hotel. They had found a church where they could go to Sunday School, and one day a Sunday School teacher said, "I am so sorry you are having so much trouble finding a home." The little girl said, "Oh, no, ma'am, we have the home, we just don't have a house to live in." Have you ever had a bad day, when everything you asked your parents for, you received a no? You wanted to go outside. No. You wanted to call someone on the phone. No. You wanted someone to come over. No. You wondered what you had done differently that day from any other day. You felt like you were being just as good. Sometimes your parents may have to tell you things like that. There are some verses in the Bible that tell us how, on those days, we ought to treat our parents and what we should remember.

Can you read the first line of this Bible verse for me? Just the first line? "Honor your father and your mother" (Exodus 20:12). Another Bible verse goes like this. Can you read that for me? "Children be obedient to your parents" (Ephesians 6:1). When they are telling you no on those days, they know what's best for you. They might also be thinking of a Bible verse for them as a parent to know how to work with you.

Mr. Williams planted two vegetable gardens. He planted a big one and a tiny one over on the side of the yard. His neighbor, Mr. Smith, kept coming over and looking at that vegetable garden, and the Smiths didn't have a vegetable garden. They were hoping they would get some things out of that other garden. In that big vegetable garden, the whole family would go out there, water it, put fertilizer on it, pull up the weeds, and they took good care of it. But they didn't do a thing to the little garden. They just left it alone.

One day Mr. Smith said, "I don't understand. Why are you taking care of this one vegetable garden, and you're not taking care of the other one?" Mr. Williams was able to look at him and say, "I have talked to you about going to church, and I want your sons and your daughters to go to church and to Sunday School, but you always say, 'let them have a choice when they get older.'" Then he said, "It's sort of like my vegetable garden. I'm taking really good care of this one vegetable garden, but look at that little bitty one there. I left it to choose what it wanted to do, and now all it has is a bunch of weeds. There isn't anything in that garden but weeds." He said, "It's because I remember that verse in the Bible for parents that I am to 'train up my children so that when they are older, they will remember what I have taught them' (Proverbs 22:6)." So, sometimes when you're getting those nos on those days, and you're not feeling really good about them, you remember what the Bible says to you - that you are to honor your mother and father, but also remember what it has to say to your parents, train up your children in the way you want them to go.

Let's pray. *Father, we are so thankful for our special parents: our own mothers and our own fathers. We know that they love us and that they care about us. Help us to practice the rule of hugging each other every day. In Jesus' Name, Amen.*

OBJECT: Pictures - Summertime Things to Do

Safe Like the "Joey"

Kangaroos are fascinating animals. We call them marsupials. That name simply means that the mother has a pouch. When a baby kangaroo is born, it's only about an inch high and weighs about one ounce, is blind, and doesn't have any fur. But that mother takes the baby kangaroo and puts it in her pouch.

A baby kangaroo is called a "joey." The baby then has the food, warmth, and security it needs. A male kangaroo is called a "boomer," and he can grow to weigh as much as 200 pounds. A mother kangaroo is called a "flyer," and I think that's a pretty good name, because she doesn't weigh as much and can run a lot faster - probably has to run after her baby more.

Kangaroos have powerful back legs, and because of that they can hop as far as twenty-five feet at a time. The mother kangaroo takes care of the baby, and there's a special verse in the Bible that tells how God meets our needs in the same way. It's found in Matthew 6:8, "Your Father already knows what you need before you ask Him." This mother knows what her baby needs: warmth, security, and closeness.

God knows what our needs are, and we must stay close to Him. Another verse goes along with this. Philippians 4:19, "And my God will meet all your needs according to his glorious riches in Christ Jesus." This mother kangaroo gives life to her baby by protecting it and making it feel safe and secure. Kangaroos are timid, but this mother will protect her baby at all costs.

God gives life to us. He promised us life everlasting (life forever), eternal life if we only believe so we then have the feeling of safety and security. This baby joey depends on its mother. We need to depend on God. As this baby kangaroo stays close to its mother, it becomes a strong and powerful animal. If we stay close to God, we will become strong and powerful Christians, feeling safe and secure in our world.

Let's pray. *Dear Father, we thank You that You know our needs and that we need only to ask. In Jesus' name, Amen.*

OBJECT: Kangaroo Pictures

One Little Boy's Lunch

Can you tell me what this is? It's a lunch bag. If I open it up, I have a sandwich (it's peanut butter) and a thermos that has some fruit in it. Suppose I ask you to stay after church with me today and eat lunch with me, and you say, "Ok, where's the food?" and I bring out this sandwich and this thermos of fruit, and you say, "Is that all the food we have?" and I say, "Yes, that's it," do you think you would have enough to eat? No. I don't think so either.

Jesus took a lunch about this size, and He did something very wonderful to it. Jesus had been with His disciples. They were very tired, they had been talking to the people, and they needed some rest. Jesus and His disciples got into a boat, and they crossed the Sea of Galilee to get away from the people for awhile. But the people saw the boat, and they knew where Jesus was going. By the time Jesus reached the other side of the sea and went up on the mountain with His disciples, all of these people were there, too. It turned out that there were not just hundreds. There were 5,000 people. Jesus didn't become angry with them for coming when He was trying to rest; He started teaching them. It was almost evening, and one of His disciples said to Jesus, "Shouldn't we send them back to the village? They need to go buy something to eat."

Jesus said, "Philip, where could we go to buy enough food to feed these people?" Philip said, "5,000 people? We can't buy food for 5,000 people." About that time, Andrew said, "There's a little boy who has a lunch, and in his lunch he has five loaves and two fish." Jesus said, "Get all the people to sit down and bring the little boy to me, and we'll share his lunch." Jesus took the bread, blessed it, He was so thankful for it (this is supposed to be a slice of bread), and He began to break it. What happened when He started breaking it? He got some more. He kept breaking it. What was happening? He had more and more food! What about when the disciples started feeding it to everyone? Did He have enough to go around? Yes, He had plenty. Then they brought the fish to

Him, and He broke them. Was there enough fish to go around? Yes, there was, because as Jesus blessed the bread and the fish, He began multiplying it, and by the time the people had finished eating, they were full. How many baskets of leftover food did they have? Twelve baskets of food were left over! Jesus took something very small and made it into something very large (see Mark 6).

In our church we sometimes hear some big words: stewardship and budget. Do you know what those words mean? They mean bringing an offering to church. You may say, "I don't have much offering to bring to church." You may have a nickel or a dime or a quarter. But what did Jesus do? He took something very small and made it into something very large. If we all bring our offering, and put it all together in the offering plate, what's going to happen? We're going to have something very large, just like Jesus was able to do with the loaves and fish.

Let's pray. *Thank You, God, for letting us give our money to our church. Thank You for letting us put something that may be very small to us, together with other people's offering, and making it very large, for we know that offering is used to tell other people about Jesus. Amen.*

OBJECTS: Bread/Fish/Lunch Pail

Look in the Mirror!

You have all seen ponds and lakes, and maybe you have seen the reflection of the sky and trees in a lake or pond. If you have, you have looked into a mirror because a mirror is anything that is smooth, where the light reflects, and you can see the image of something else there.

But do you know what happens when the breeze blows on that lake and it begins to have waves and to ruffle up? You can't see the sky and trees in the lake anymore. It still reflects the light, but you can't see the images because a mirror, for it to reflect, has to be very smooth. We have found out through digging in other countries, that over 2,000 years before Christ was born, the Egyptians found out what mirrors or images were like. They took things like this brass and made it into a mirror. If you look into it, you don't see the kind of image you are used to seeing. You can't see your face as clearly, can you? But this is what they used. Sometimes, too, they would take silver and use it as a mirror.

Then some people in another country began to take glass, heat it, blow it, and make it flat. They began to have a different kind of mirror. But it wasn't until about 150 years ago that a German scientist, Justus Bleibig, took a piece of glass and made the kind of mirror we have now. You take a simple pane of glass like you would have in a window, but you put a special coating of aluminum, silver, or chromium on the back of it. The glass is not what causes you to see yourself. It's that aluminum on the backside. The glass is simply serving as a protection so you don't scratch up that silver or aluminum.

Have you ever watched little babies in the nursery when they first find out about a mirror? They will crawl up to that mirror and pick at it. They are not really sure what they are seeing. My dog is sort of like that, too. She gets in front of a mirror, and she starts barking because she thinks she is seeing another dog in the room.

People used to be very superstitious about mirrors. They thought that was their spirit in there, and that's why they say if you break a mirror you will have seven years of bad luck. We all have a mirror that we use, and I'm sure that all of you have used it many times a day. If I hold this up and you look into it, you are going to see yourself in it. Some of your friends who are down here all want to make sure they see themselves in it. Can you see? If you look into it, you are going to see that you don't look like anyone else.

We all have eyes and ears and a nose and hair, but we all look very different. But what is so special is that God made you different, and He made you special. So don't sit around and say, "I wish I were like somebody else." Sit around and say, "I'm glad

I'm who I am, because God made me that way. If I want to be different, help me to change to be just a little better."

There is a verse in the Bible, 1 Corinthians 7:7, where Paul said, "Each has his or her own special gift from God, one of one kind and one of another." As you look into this mirror, you see what your special gift is from God. Your special gift is that God made you different. He made you the you that you see in this mirror.

Let's pray. *Thank You, God, for making us different, but for making us very special. Help us as we look at ourselves each day to try to be better, to be that better person that you made us to be. Amen.*

OBJECT: Mirror

All of Us Are Getting Older

I'm going to hold up pictures with me this morning and see if you can tell me who they remind you of. Does anybody have an idea who these remind them of? Maybe grandparents? Grandmother and grandfather? Does this remind you of anybody else? How about some older friends you have? Do any of you have older friends who are not grandparents?

I remember as a child getting to visit my grandparents. We would have to travel for a whole day to reach them. I thought we'd never get to their farm, but we finally did. Sometimes in the summer it would be so special because I would be able to stay and visit with them two or three weeks. I want you to look at this picture. This is a real picture. Who do you think that is a photograph of? This is a picture of my grandparents. You've heard parents and different people say, "Oh, you look just like your mother," or, "Oh, you're just like your father." Well, sometimes, they even say, "You look just like your grandparents." A very special time would be when my grandfather would come in out of the fields, and he would sit in a big, red rocking chair we had, and he would put on these glasses. Do these look anything like glasses that you've seen today? They don't look like yours, do they? They certainly don't look anything like contacts. But he would put on these glasses, and he would sit in that rocking chair, and rock, and he would read the evening newspaper. Do you know when the best time was? He would say, "Come on and sit in my lap, and I'll read you a story." Maybe your grandparents read to you, too. Do any of your grandparents live near you? How many of you have grandparents who live in other places? Sometimes they live far away, and you have to go visit them, don't you? Grandparents are great. Sometimes we have older friends who are also very special, and they are not our grandparents. Think about an older friend you might have who lives down the street.

There was a young man who began painting when he was thirteen years old, but his most famous painting was painted when he was ninety years old. He lived in a faraway country called Italy. He painted this ceiling of the chapel. Can you see the picture? He painted this ceiling and the walls, and it took him four years to paint this. He had to lie on his back for four years, but he painted it when he was ninety! That's a pretty hard job for someone who is ninety years old, isn't it?

As we are thinking about grandparents and older adults, I want you to think of ways you can share with them. Perhaps you can write a letter to your grandparents if they live out of town, and you can tell them about something you did yesterday. Maybe you had a soccer game. Maybe you have a baseball game you are working really hard to win. Maybe you have a new doll with new clothes, and you had a special tea party with that doll, and you want to tell your grandparents about it. Some of you can pick up the phone and call them. Some of us are lucky enough to have our grandparents visiting with us today, aren't we? You can share a lot with your grandparents today. Let's think about ways we can show our grandparents and our older friends that we really care about them.

Let's pray. *Thank You, God, for Your plan for us to become older. Thank You for grandparents. Thank You for older friends who are very special to us. Amen.*

OBJECT: Pictures of Older People/Picture of Michelangelo and Sistine Chapel

Jesus' Pupils

I have many objects that I am going to hold up, and I imagine that as I hold them up, you will know why. Here's some paper, a pencil, a ruler, and some crayons. Why? Because everybody's been going back to school, haven't they? Your school may be day-care, kindergarten, preschool, or you may have started to first grade this year. You may be in second, third, fourth, fifth, or sixth grades, but you know what those objects are, and you have so many beautiful books to look at and to learn from. Think of all the workbooks you have. You have many reading books to study in your different grades, math books, and science books, and you have many opportunities to learn very well.

Did you ever stop and think about children going to school back in Bible times? They did. In the Old Testament a teacher was called, not a teacher, but "wise." Instead of your being called students or pupils, you would be called "disciples". In the time of the New Testament when Jesus was born, a teacher was called a "rabbi." You don't go into your teacher and say, "Good morning, Rabbi," or "Good morning, Master." You say, "Good morning, Teacher."

Do you think Jesus went to school? Yes, He did. How do we know that? In Luke 2:52 it says, "Jesus grew in wisdom." That means He studied and learned. Jesus went to a church school called a synagogue. He lived in a little town called Nazareth. Instead of there being many schools like today, they had one school, so Jesus and all His friends went to the synagogue school in Nazareth.

When Jesus was twelve, He went with His parents to Jerusalem for some holy days, and as they came back, His parents found that Jesus was not with them. They returned and found Jesus in the temple, praying. He was also talking to the scribes and the priests, and He understood what all the grownups were talking about. People were saying, "Who is this boy? How does he at twelve understand all of the things that the grown people understand?" Jesus worked very hard and learned because He knew that throughout His life He would be asked questions He needed to know how to explain.

Remember when He taught His twelve disciples? He taught them, sent them out, and told them to teach. Jesus was the greatest teacher we ever had. He didn't just talk to adults, though. Do you remember in the Bible where He said, "Let the little children come to me," because He wanted to teach children as well? He taught children about God's love. He taught us what we can do to please God. He taught us how we should live. Do you know that Jesus is still teaching us today? Do you know how He is still teaching us? When you study your Bible, Jesus is teaching you how you should live. There's another Bible verse that goes along with what we are talking about this morning, "Study to show thyself approved unto God" (2 Timothy 2:15). Jesus studied hard because He wanted God to approve of what He did, just as you need to study hard so God will approve of what you do, so that you, too, will grow in wisdom as Jesus did.

Let's pray. *Thank You, God, for giving us minds that are able to learn. Help us to realize that we can learn not only at school, but at home and at church. We thank You for Your Bible which teaches us to live as Jesus wants us to live. Amen.*

OBJECTS: Various Books

Lifeless Without God

I have a little hand puppet with me. If I hold this little puppet up, it doesn't do anything. Lifeless, isn't it? If I put my hands inside this puppet, suddenly its little feet can move, it can twitch its nose, and I could keep it here in the palm of my hand where you almost think it is real.

Here's a glove. It doesn't do anything unless I put my hand inside it. Then it does what a glove can do. It can make a fist; it can be feet that walk. I can reach in my basket and pick up a pencil.

These things require that I put my hand inside them; this puppet is lifeless without my hand, this glove is limp without my hand. God looks at us as being like this puppet or glove, and until we ask Him to come into our lives and be a part of us, we're just as lifeless and as limp as this glove. When we ask Him to come into our lives, the Holy Spirit comes and lives in our hearts. Suddenly we know how to love people, how to care for each other, and we know what peace and joy are all about. The next time you have a puppet at school or home, or on a cold day when you put on your mittens or gloves, think about the power of the Holy Spirit—that hand coming inside the glove. In Acts 1:8 we read, "Ye shall receive power after the Holy Spirit is come upon you." We must trust Jesus for the Holy Spirit to live within us.

Let's pray. *Dear Father, we do want to believe in You. Help us to do that so the Holy Spirit can make things very wonderful and special. In Jesus' name. Amen.*

OBJECTS: Hand Puppet/Glove/Pencil

Don't be Something You're Not

Do you remember how Tom Sawyer got the neighborhood boys to paint the fence? He pretended it was going to be something that was a whole lot of fun, so they all began to paint. We paint for many reasons. Sometimes we paint because we need to hide dust because we haven't taken care of the rooms as well as we should have. Sometimes we're trying to hide other things like cracks or water stains in the ceiling. Painting can be something that is a lot of work.

Before Jesus' time there was a black slave by the name of Aesop. Aesop was a very educated man. We remember him because of the stories (fables) he told to children and adults. The story goes that one time Jupiter, who was a god, decided he wanted to decide which bird was going to be king over all other birds. He asked the birds to get ready, to fly before him, and he would pick the one who would be king. So all the birds were preening their feathers and trying to get as good-looking as they could, but the jackdaw knew he didn't have a single chance, because he was so ugly. As the feathers fell out onto the ground, he thought, I have an idea. I'll take those feathers that the other birds are taking out and I'll put them on me so I'll have a beautiful plumage. So the jackdaw flew in front of Jupiter. Jupiter was just about to say, "you will be the king of all the birds." Just then the other birds realized what he had done. They stripped the feathers off the jackdaw. The bird tried to be something that it wasn't.

Shakespeare wrote, "All that glitters is not gold." In my basket, I have a cabbage. If you look at this cabbage, it's pretty much like it was when it came from the grocery store. But as I start peeling off these leaves, what am I going to have down below? More leaves. I can peel this until church is over, and what am I going to have all the way down? Leaves. That's what I think is really neat about a cabbage. Cabbage is the same thing on the outside as it is on the inside. That's how God wants us to be.

Sometimes you're busy doing nice things for people on the outside, being kind and good, but you know what you're thinking on the inside? Why am I having to do this? I didn't want to do this in the first place. This cabbage is the same on the inside as it is on the outside as God would have us to be. Philippians 4:8 says,

"Finally ... whatever is true, whatever is noble, whatever is right, whatever is pure, whatever is lovely, whatever is admirable, if anything is excellent or praiseworthy, think about these things."

Let's pray. *Dear Father, help us to really be what we appear to be - that we're the same on the outside as well as on the inside. Amen.*

OBJECT: Cabbage

Learning from a Spider

I brought a riddle book with me this morning. All of the riddles rhyme. Let's see if you can figure this one out. What did Sam find swimming in his apple cider? Why rhymes? Cider. What rhymes? Spider. These creatures have eight legs on them. I can't get into telling you about all different kinds of spiders, because there are 30,000 different kinds of spiders. In one acre of ground, you might find as many as 2.2 million spiders. A mother spider can carry as many as 600 on her back at one time, and they don't fall off.

I want to share a fable with you this morning. Once there was a spider who wanted to build a nest in a barn. He went up to the very top rafter, looked down, and said, "I see a perfect place to build my web." He put that first line down from that very top rafter. It looked so thin and delicate, and we think, How could that spider walk on it? but he could. Finally, he reached the place where he wanted to build his web. He started spinning out other lines (spokes), attaching them to other parts of the barn. Then he ran around in a big circle and began to make the part of the web that holds it all together. It wasn't finished yet. He came back and did another big spin circle, this time with a sticky type of thread. He sat back and thought, Boy this is a fine web. This is going to catch me a lot of flies. I'm going to be able to eat and live here happily. Well, sure enough he did. He got fat, content, and sassy. One day he started walking about this web, and he went back and said, What is that long line attached all the way to that top rafter? Why did I put it there? It doesn't help me catch any flies. It's of no use. Wonder why I did that? Immediately, he decided to break that line. What happened? The web collapsed. The spider wasn't thinking, and he forgot that was his important link back to where he started from.

I want us to think about our important link, our link with God who gives us strength. You have a friend at school who you talk to. You have a friend you like to call on the phone. That's called a conversation, isn't it? I have another riddle, and I know you're going to know it. I have a special friend I can talk to morning, noon, night, in my bedroom, in the kitchen, when I'm mowing the grass, when I'm happy, when I'm sad, when I'm afraid. Who am I talking about? You're with Him today. God. All right.

In my conversation with God I'm talking to God. But the neat thing is we know that when we talk to God He is going to listen and hear us. We have prayers in our service. God will hear each one of those and listen. Hear this verse found in Jeremiah 29:12, "You will call upon me and come and pray to me, and I will listen to you." The spider tore down his link to the top beam. Let's keep our link connected to God through our conversation and prayer time with Him.

Let's pray. *Dear Father, thank You that You love each one of us, Your people. Thank You for letting us have conversations with You, talking to You, and know You will listen. Amen.*

OBJECT: Book

Can We Help Jesus?

Yes, this is a milk carton. It's empty now, isn't it? Before I could go to the grocery store, buy this carton of milk and use it, many people had to work to get this on the shelf in the store. Somebody had to feed that baby calf. Somebody had to be sure that those cows got out to pasture, because they need green grass to eat. The cows can't always be outside in the green pasture, can they? They've got to have food in the winter when there is no pasture. Somebody has to bale that hay and put it into the barn. Then, they take the cows and milk them in the milking parlor. Once that cow is milked, it is put into cans, and it waits for the milk truck to come. Here's the milk truck. All that milk is loaded on this milk truck. It's taken to the plant in the city. In the city many people help to pasteurize that milk and put it into containers so your parents can go to the store and buy that milk for you. Do you see that it took a lot of people to get that milk to the store for us?

Jesus needed many people to help Him, too. He knew He couldn't do His work by himself. He needed many helpers, and many friends. Jesus went down to the Sea of Galilee, and as He was walking along the beach, He saw two fishermen who had cast their nets. Their names were Simon, who was called Peter, and Andrew. "Simon Peter and Andrew, will you come with Me? Will you be My helpers? Will you be My friends? Come, and I will make you fishers of men." That meant He wanted them to help.

He went farther on down the beach and saw some more fishermen. They were seated in a boat with their father, Zebedee. Their names were James and John. They were seated in the boat because they were having to mend their nets, because in catching fish, their nets had torn. While they were sitting there mending their nets, Jesus asked, "James and John, will you follow Me? Will you come and be My helpers?" They immediately followed Jesus.

Then He went on into the town of Capernaum. There He met a man named Matthew, a tax collector. You know what taxes are. If you want to buy something for $1, you must have (put your rate) for the tax. "Matthew, will you come and follow Me, too?" Jesus kept going until He had twelve disciples who would follow Him. They were Jesus' helpers (see Matthew 10:1-4).

See if you can count them on your fingers with me. There were twelve disciples Jesus called to help Him. Simon Peter, Andrew, James, his brother John, Philip, Thomas, Matthew, James, the son of Alphaeus, Thaddeus, Simon, Judas, and Bartholomew. These helpers worked with Jesus while He was here on earth. When He left, He told them to teach, preach, and to baptize. Jesus is not here with us on earth, and His first disciples are not here now.

Who are Jesus' helpers today? Us. That's right. We are Jesus' helpers. We are here on earth to help carry out His work. Do you know how we can help Jesus today? By coming to Sunday School and worship, by bringing friends who live on the street with us, friends from school, kinfolks, and we can also be Jesus' helpers by giving our money to our church.

Let's pray. *Thank You, God, that we can be Jesus' friends. Thank You for letting us be His helpers here today. Thank You for letting us give our money which reaches out and helps many people. In Your Name we pray, Amen.*

OBJECT: Milk Carton

Faithfulness Finds Golds

It happened awhile back. A man named Mr. Peters had a hardware company called Peters Hardware. He was a wealthy man, but it seemed like there was always a sign in his window that said, "Boy Wanted." Many boys went in to apply for the job, but they didn't stay very long. The first boy who came in was named Frank Adams. Frank worked for half of the morning, delivering hardware items to different people who called. Mr. Peters then said, "Frank, I want you to go up in the attic. I have a big wooden box up there full of stuff, and I want you to go through it." Frank did. It was kind of cold, and there were spider webs there. He thought he heard mice scurrying around. He looked in that box and thought, Uh, there's nothing any good in there, and I'm not wasting my time on that box. So he came back downstairs and said, "Mr. Peters, I was hired to be an errand boy." Mr. Peters just smiled and said, "Well,

I really hired you to do anything I asked you to do." That day he paid him his salary and said he wouldn't need him the next day.

The second fellow who came to apply for the job was Sammy Pittman. By afternoon, Mr. Peters said, "Sammy, there's a wooden box up in the attic. I need you to go up in the attic, and I want you to go through it." Well, Sammy wasn't afraid of the spiders, the cobwebs, or the mice. He didn't think it was too cold, but he looked in that box and thought, Uh, there's nothing any good in here. He kind of raked his hand around in it, picked out one or two things, brought them downstairs, gave them to Mr. Peters, and said, "This's all I could find that was any good." Mr. Peters just smiled, and at the end of the day he paid him his salary and said he wouldn't need him the next day.

The third young man was Willard Smith. Willard didn't get upstairs the first day, but he got upstairs the second day. Mr. Peters told him the same thing. Well, Willard stayed up there all morning Mr. Peters called and said, "Willard, aren't you going to come down and eat lunch?" Willard answered, "Oh, sir, there is still so much for me to do up here." Mr. Peters said, "Oh, come on down anyway." Then Willard went back up and stayed all afternoon. Mr. Peters thought, What is that young fellow doing upstairs in that attic with that box?

When Willard came down, held out his hand, and said, "Mr. Peters, I've done everything I knew to do, and guess what I found in the bottom of this box? There is a five dollar gold piece. That's a strange place for it to be." Mr. Peter smiled, put it in his pocket, and said, "I'll see you in the morning, Willard." Mr. Peters went upstairs to his attic. The box now had compartments in it. Willard had taken some wood he found in the attic and made compartments, and they were labeled. They said, washers, bolts, screws, picture hangers. Willard had gone through everything in that box, and he had found and categorized them.

To make this story shorter, Willard became the errand boy for Mr. Peters. Mr. Peters gave him a sign to put up in his bedroom that said, "He that is faithful in that which is least is faithful also in much." Mr. Peters also said, "Son, this is your future." Willard became the Smith in Peters, Smith & Company. He became a partner in the company.

I doubt that there's any place around this church where there's going to be a five dollar gold piece buried. Wishful thinking. But we will see what all I do have. A bag, Tinkertoys, wire, old papers; I think I could really throw these away: a brown piece of cork, a Viewmaster, and I promise this was in there. You know if you look at this, boys and girls, this is your future. This is your Bible, your guide to your Christian life. Let's look at Luke 16:10, "Whosoever is faithful in small matters will be faithful in large ones."

Let's pray. *Dear Father, help us to be faithful in doing those small tasks at hand. Help us to be those kinds of Christians in our day-to-day work. Amen.*

OBJECTS: A Bag / Tinkertoys / Wire / Papers / Cork / Viewmaster / Bible

Putting Humpty-Dumpty Together Again

How many of you have ever had a broken bone—arm or leg? I've had a broken nose. How many of you in the last week or two might have had a fight with a brother, sister, mother, or father? How many of you have lost someone very special in your life because they died? I know several of you have lost some grandparents recently, haven't you? Last week when I was in the Child Development Center, the boys and girls in the Two and Three Year Old Class were learning nursery rhymes, and they are always so proud they can say one. This is one they repeated to me:

Humpty-Dumpty sat on a wall.
Humpty-Dumpty had a great fall.

All the king's horses and all the king's men.
Couldn't put Humpty-Dumpty together again.

In the literal sense of the word Humpty-Dumpty was an egg. He sat on a wall. He fell off and broke into many pieces. He couldn't be put back together again. If I take an egg and crack it in this bowl, do you think I would be able to put all the pieces together again? I don't think so either, I could try as hard as I wanted to, to put that yolk and white back into that egg, but I could never get all those broken pieces back together again.

What in the world does that egg and Humpty-Dumpty have to do with church and the message of Jesus? That's a pretty good question, isn't it? Remember that men and women fell out of their relationship with God, and God was not real happy about that, so He sent His Son, Jesus, to show us how to come back into a right relationship with Him. In sending His Son, Jesus, Jesus then became the glue that was going to put all the broken pieces of our lives together again.

You know that when your arm or leg is broken, it mends, but it may not always feel the same. When Jesus came, He showed us how to live in relationship with God. When we have fights with our brothers and sisters, we can go back to Jesus' life and see how He lived and how He solved problems. You also know that in the gospel of Jesus He died on a cross.

God's love should be pasted in our hearts always, because we realize that God loved us so much He let His son die for us on the cross so we would never be separated or broken apart again. Then the most special part of the gospel message is that Jesus rose out of the tomb. He didn't stay there. He entered into a new life. He stuck together with God, God stuck with Him, and they were one. Isn't that a wonderful message to think about? No matter how broken our lives may become or how much of a mess we have made of them, Jesus then can put us all back together, unlike this egg that can never be put together again.

John 11:25 says, "I am the resurrection and the life. He who believes in me shall live, even if he dies." So Jesus then becomes our glue who holds us together now and forever, if we only believe.

Let's pray. *Dear Father, we thank You anew for Your love for us. Help us to accept us Your way in putting our pieces back together again. Amen.*

OBJECTS: Egg/Bowl

Idioms, Not Idiots

There are three "idioms" I want to talk to you about this morning. An idiom is when a phrase brings really funny pictures to our minds. The first one - and I hope you heard it this week at school - is, "My, you did a good job. You passed that test with flying colors!" See the picture I drew. It doesn't really mean that, does it? I have another one. "She has a frog in her throat." The main one I want to talk to you about this morning is one in the Bible, "The apple of his eyes." Does that mean we are talking about apples? Or eyes?

Eyes are important, but small. They are carefully made and complicated. You have heard the words pupil, iris, retina, and cornea. You know our eyes work a lot like a camera or movie screen. The most important part I want us to look at this morning is the pupil - the very center of the eye. Whatever we look at comes in through that pupil. It flashes back on that movie screen, the waves go up to our brain, and we look at that picture. We either react happy or sad to it, or we may have no reaction at all. The pupil is the most important part - the very center of the eye.

The English people think it is so important that they call it "the apple of their eye." God told the people in Israel they were special to Him, that He loved them so much. When the English were trying to translate the Bible from Hebrew into English, they wanted a really great word to show God's love. They tried to find a special word or phrase, and finally came up with this idiom: "The apple of his eye." We find that verse in Deuteronomy 32:10, "God protected them as though they were the apple of his eye." Each one of us is the apple of God's eye. He loves us, He cares for us, and He continues to have that pupil centered straight on us.

Let's pray. *Dear Father, help each one of us to share Your love this week. Amen.*

OBJECTS: Idioms/Pictures

"Put on a Happy Face"

What are these? Candy wrappers. Why do you think they are around a candy bar? To protect it? Also, they are a way of advertising. Hershey's hasn't changed their wrappers in years. All of us who are chocolate lovers know what a Hershey wrapper looks like, don't we? It's there for advertisement as much as it is to hold it together. If I hold these up, what are they? Book covers. They used to call them dust covers, and they called them dust covers because they kept dust off the books. Somebody might call them a book wrapper, because they are wrapped around a book.

If you saw this book in the library, you might not get real excited about checking it out. It's just a plain, old book. But if it had this cover on it, you might say, "Hey, I might want to look at that. There's something about Mickey Mouse on it, and there's Minnie. This looks like it's fun." So the book cover is there sometimes to make you want to check out the book, to advertise, to make it look exciting inside. Sometimes you might have a good-looking book cover, and you might check out the book and find out that it's pretty dull. That's why we came by the saying, "You can't judge a book by its cover." Shakespeare also said that "all that glitters is not gold." Just because it looks like gold on the outside, on the inside it may not be.

Think about your face. "Physiognomy" is a big word just to say that by looking at your face many of you let people know what you are thinking. Do they read truth in your face or do you give them the wrong impression? Think about houses whose yards look so nice. But with the pretty flowers in the yards and the fresh painting on the outside, the house looks good. Then you might get inside and find it really dirty and musty. You can't always tell about a house by its outside either, can you?

There was a missionary in China whom the boys and girls called "Mr. Happy Face." They called him that because they said his face was happy on the outside, but they knew that he was happy on the inside, that he loved them. That was a big compliment.

Have you ever heard of someone called Calamity Jane? Calamity Jane on the outside looked like a wreck. She was a woman of the Wild West in the Black Hills of South Dakota. Calamity means trouble, and people said, "Oh, she got her name because she's always in trouble." One of my favorite stories about her is when she went into a town called Hill City. There was a village there, but across the stream there was another house. She asked who lived in it, and the people said an old man, his wife, and their children. "We haven't seen them in a few weeks because they have scarlet fever." Calamity Jane asked, "Then nobody is going over there to take care of them?" She pulled her gun out of its holster, held it on the man in the general store, and said, "You fill these baskets with food." Then she held her gun on some men and said, "Now you carry these baskets across the stream." Calamity Jane went over to those people, and she stayed with them and nursed them back to health. Some people said, "Calamity maybe means that she helps people who are in trouble." You can't always judge a book by its cover. She really had a lot down inside.

Think about Jesus and His disciples. Jesus breathed the Holy Spirit on those disciples. They had sparkles in their eyes, a firm handshake, and determined steps. But there was something inside them that attracted people, as well as on the outside, and that drew them to Jesus. Are you a Christian only on the outside or is that

Christian also on the inside? Do you come to church, then go home, cheat your neighbor, or tell a lie over the phone? Or is that Christian totally on the inside? Can they judge you by your cover? Do we look at what's on the inside?

Let's pray. *Dear Father, help us to be faithful. Help us to be exciting inside as well as out. Amen.*

OBJECTS: Candy Wrappers/Book Covers

Turning Bad into Good

Soap as we know it today is partly the result of an accident. During the Civil War, Proctor and Gamble, which was a small firm in Cincinnati, Ohio, had the contract for making all the candles and all the soap for the army. With such a small firm they had to work twenty-four hours a day, and they had to invent more machines to make more soap. One day it happened. A night-shift operator fell asleep on the job, the mixture was overwhipped, and the bars of soap were filled with air. The manager, trying to save things, came back and said, "Let's put it all back in the kettle, boil it again, and see if we can't make something out of this mess." Somebody else said, "No, let's go ahead and send the bars out. Maybe the customers will like it." So they sent this Ivory Soap out, whipped with air. Many, many orders started coming in up and down the Ohio River. "We like that new soap. It floats in the water. Please send it to us." They called it the white soap.

One Sunday morning in 1859 Harley Proctor was in church, but his mind wasn't where it should have been. He was thinking about his Ivory Soap (he hadn't named it that yet). It was "white soap." Suddenly the preacher read a verse from the Psalms. It said, "All thy garments smell of myrrh," and it went on to say another thing, " . . . out of the ivory palaces" (Psalm 45:8). Suddenly Harley Proctor said, "I have a name for my white soap. I'm going to call it Ivory." He sent a lot of bars around to different chemists and laboratories to see if it measured up to the standards of other fine soaps on the market. One chemist wrote back and said, "It's 99.44% pure. It floats." That became one of the biggest advertising slogans in all of American history. Good things can come out of bad things.

You remember all the bad things Paul was doing to the Christians? Suddenly he had a conversion experience. You would expect good things to happen to Paul, but they didn't. Bad things continued to happen. He got into trouble with the authorities. There were towns where he was told he could not come back. There were places he was told he could not preach. This sounds like maybe he wasn't doing a good job of spreading the gospel, doesn't it? But Paul firmly believed that God had control of his life and that God knew how to make good things come from bad. In fact, Paul was so sure of that that when he was in prison at Rome, he wrote a letter to the Philippians. This is what he said, "What has happened to me has really served to advance the gospel" (Philippians 1:12). God is still in control. He knows how to take those bad things and turn them into good.

Let's pray. *Dear Father, help us to let You have control of our lives. Help us to take those bad things and turn them around for good. Amen.*

OBJECT: Ivory Soap

God's Jewels

I imagine a lot of you have had to clean out closets, shelves, and toy chests because you probably got some new toys over the holidays. I even tried to clean off my desk a little bit; it has stacks of paper on top of it and stacks of paper beside it. As I was doing some cleaning, I found a story I want to share with you this morning. It's a story I heard on one of my trips, and it took place many years ago in Sterling, Scotland.

One Sunday afternoon had been planned for all the boys and girls who went to church in the area to come to the central church in that little Scottish village to have a service. Boys and girls came from all around. They opened the church doors, and the pews were packed. There was no room left. Some boys and girls had to sit up and down the aisles and on the floor, even on the steps leading up to the pulpit. They had to sit near the pulpit, and they had to sit in the choirloft because there was no other space. They had a prayer, sang a song, someone read a Bible verse, and then Reverend Robertson got up.

He said that the Bible is like a tree with many branches, and each one of those branches is one of the sixty-six books of the Bible. On each branch we have twigs, and they represent the chapters in that Book of the Bible. If you put leaves on each of the twigs, those leaves would stand for each of the verses. He went on to explain to the boys and girls that if you said, the "forty-third branch on the tree," you would be talking about John's Gospel. Then Reverend Robertson said, "I've got one I want you to figure out. How about the thirty-ninth branch, the third twig, and the seventeenth leaf?" The children got in their Bibles and started looking really fast trying to be the first to find it.

One of the young boys, who had been seated behind the minister, stood up and put his finger in the Bible. Reverend Robertson said, "You did find it! You found Malachi, the last Book in the Old Testament, the thirty-ninth branch. Son, I would like for you to go up into the pulpit, and I would like for you to read the Scripture verse, clearly and slowly, so that everyone can understand it." So this young boy did that, and these are the words he read: "Thou shalt be mine in that day when I make up my jewels." When the boy finished, Reverend Robertson said, "Son, someday I hope you will be a pastor yourself."

Well, the young boy didn't grow up to be a pastor, but he preached and lectured all over the world, and many young men who heard him became pastors. You might want to know his name. His name was Henry Drummond, and many of your parents and grandparents will be really familiar with the little book (you aren't quite old enough to have read this book yet) called *The Greatest Thing in the World.* This is a book he wrote. He was a scientist, but he was a Christian and approached things in a much different way than people did in the 1800s.

This minister that day was talking about a tree, branches, twigs, and leaves. Let's look at that verse one more time which Henry Drummond read that day. "They shall be mine in that day when I make up my jewels." Who are God's jewels? YOU are God's jewels. You are not kids in God's eyes. You are not little monsters like we sometimes think you are. You are something very precious to Him. You are very valuable jewels.

Sometimes parents give you names that represent jewels: Ruby, Opal, Pearl. You might be named Margaret, which means pearl. Boys might be named Garnet or Diamond. Your mother might have called you her precious little pet when you were much smaller or her precious little jewel. As you are now growing older, I want each one of you to realize that this verse from Malachi says that YOU are God's precious jewels—each one very valuable to Him.

Let's pray. *Dear Father, help us to love You more each day so we may be shining, bright jewels, precious in Your sight. Amen.*

OBJECT: Book: *The Greatest Thing in the World*

Seeing Through the Eyes of Faith

The magnifying glass was not invented until about 300 years ago. There were so many neat things we could see suddenly because we had a magnifying glass. Do you know that over half the plants in the whole world cannot be seen with just our naked eye? There are thousands and thousands of tiny little animal forms we cannot see unless we have a magnifying glass.

This special glass is curved, is thicker in the center, and gets thinner as it comes out toward the edges. The way the light shines through the glass makes things underneath it appear much larger. Many of you have these at home, and I know you have probably gotten some pond water and used your magnifying glass to look at it, or a feather, a strand of your own hair, seashells from the beach, or even a plain old rock to see what you could discover.

We can't see God with our naked eye either, can we? How do we find out discoveries about God? First of all, we find out by reading our Bible. Many, many things about God are told to us by our Bible, but we also find out discoveries about God as we pray with to Him.

Do you remember when you were little? The hardest thing for you to learn to do was to tie shoelaces. We are really lucky now because so many of our tennis shoes have velcro. Many of us said, "I don't want to wear any shoes," because we couldn't tie them. Sometimes when we put them on, we put them on the wrong feet. Or if we finally got them on the right feet, we just couldn't lace those shoes up and get them tied properly. There was usually somebody we could go to—many of us would go to our mother really frustrated and say, "Show me one more time how to tie these shoelaces." Finally we learned to tie them, but we knew we had to go to someone who could give us help.

There is a story in Mark 9:14 about a father who had a young boy who was very sick, and the father didn't know what to do. He came to the disciples and said, "I need help." The disciples said, "Let's go to someone; let's go to Jesus." So the disciples brought the father to Jesus. Jesus looked at the father and His disciples, and He said, "I need help." You know what Jesus did? He prayed. He knew that He needed to go to someone for help. So we find out that we can discover things about God. We can see Him more clearly if we pray. We also find out that we can go to God for help. We must also remember to go to Him in thanksgiving and praise.

There was a church in South Dakota that had been through a bad drought; they had not had any rain. The church got together to pray for rain. One of the children came walking into the church and down the aisle, swinging her umbrella. Someone said, "Why in the world did you bring your umbrella?'' The little girl said, ''I brought my umbrella because we came to pray for rain. If we pray, we need to have faith that it's going to happen.''

I like us to say that we are talking not to God, but that we are talking with God, because I think that means we are willing to listen when He answers us.

Let's pray. *Dear Father, thank You for letting us talk with You any place, anytime, and about anything. Amen.*

OBJECT: Magnifying Glass

Popcorn and You

Popcorn is the oldest of the three kinds of corn we know - there is field corn, which we feed to cattle and pigs; sweet corn, which we eat; and popcorn. Popcorn was discovered by the American Indians many thousands of years ago. In fact, when Columbus first came to the new world, one of the sights he saw in San Salvador was the Indians wearing jewelry made out of popcorn. A few years ago some archaeologists in New Mexico found a cave that bats had lived in for years, and they found some kernels of popcorn that were expected to be 5,000 years old. In Peru recently they found some popcorn kernels that were 1,000 years old, and they still popped! They used to have popcorn soup, and the Pilgrims even put some in a bowl, put cream on it, and ate it for breakfast!

In the United States we eat 500,000,000 pounds of popcorn a year. Thirty percent of that is eaten at movies, ball games, circuses, and fairs. Ten percent of it is saved for seeds so we can have popcorn again and sell it to other countries. Sixty percent of it is eaten in the home.

How does popcorn pop? Inside each little kernel, there is some moisture and some water, which makes a pulp. Then it has a hard outer shell, and when the popcorn is heated it causes that moisture to become steam. Suddenly it just pops open. If there is no moisture left in the kernels, we have the leftovers in the bottom of the bowl which didn't pop.

I think popcorn is delicious. Many of you probably make your own nowadays, because of these new little microwave popcorn packs you can buy. Did you know that when you are eating popcorn you are eating a vegetable?

As Christians we have something very special inside us, and that is the love of Jesus. Because we have the love of Jesus inside us, we ought to be very happy and joyful. Many times as Christians we are not, and we wonder why. Let's think about this popcorn: hard, shelled popcorn. It has to have heat under it before it becomes fluffy and before it really tastes good to eat. That's what has to happen to us as Christians. We have to let the love of Jesus so warm us that we become loving and caring, and we begin to blossom. The next time you pop your corn, I want you to look at each of these blossoms. They look a whole lot alike, don't they? But if you look at them closely, you'll see that they have popped, every one of them, a little differently. That's what happens to you as a Christian. Each one of you will become a blossom, very unique, with your own gifts and your own talents.

One of the neatest things to me about popcorn is watching it pop. One of the special things we get to do here in our church is to watch you blossom as Christians, becoming what Christ wants you to become. There is a Bible verse I want to share with you. Colossians 2:9, "You have been given full life, blossoming life, in union with Christ Jesus."

Let's pray. *Dear Father, help each one of us to be warmed by Your love and become full, blossoming Christians as You would have us to be. Amen.*

OBJECT: Popcorn

Making the Impossible Possible

I have in my hand a dime, a quarter, and a sheet of paper. I've have cut a hole out of the paper. Which coin do you think is going to go through that hole? The dime, because it looks like the smaller coin, doesn't it? Do you think I can get that quarter through the hole? Let's see if I can. Some of you think it's impossible. Let's see if I can get that quarter through that hole. Did it come through? It wasn't impossible because I knew how to do it. The quarter came through a hole that seemed only big enough for the dime.

I also have a potato. You all like to eat potatoes—fried, mashed, baked—probably you like them fried better than any other way. Do you think I can take this straw and put it into that potato? I'm pushing. Is it going in? It's not, is it? It's just a raw potato. But I am going to take this straw and cut it in two pieces. Now do you think I can push it in like this? Still not going into that potato? All of a sudden it went in. It looked like it was impossible. You may think I did something tricky to that straw. I want you to be sure there's nothing in the straw. Okay. Did it go in? Sure.

Things that seem to be impossible are not impossible if you know how to do them. That's sometimes true in our lives. We think things are impossible.

Jesus gave us a wonderful verse in Luke 18:27, "Things that are impossible with men are possible with God." What does that have to do with you as preschoolers and children? Suppose you have a boy down the street that you absolutely cannot stand, and you don't even want to be with him. You might have someone in your Sunday School class or your class at school like that. But, God told us that we should love everyone. You say, "I can't stand that guy! I don't want to be around him!" God still told us to love everyone (John 15:17). I said all things are possible with God. What do you need to do? You need to pray to God and say something like this, "God, you know I don't like that boy, but you told me that I'm supposed to love everyone and get along with them. So please help me learn how to like that person." It's not going to happen overnight. You are not, all of a sudden, the next day going to go down your block, and say, "Hey, I love you. Come play with me." It won't happen like that. But with God, those things become possible.

Let me give you another example. Maybe you don't like to do your chores around the house. Maybe you have trouble getting along with your brothers and sisters, or maybe sometimes something has happened in your life which made you very unhappy and very sad, and you don't know how to get past that. With God those things become possible if we ask for His help.

Let's pray. _Dear Father, help us to realize that we can ask for Your help in solving our problems and through difficult times. Help us to depend upon You. Amen._

OBJECTS: Dime/Quarter/Potato

Recharging Our Batteries

If I hold this up, who can tell me what this is? It's a battery. It takes five of these batteries, D-cells, to make this flashlight work. I'm going to finish putting these batteries in here, and then we'll see what happens. It took those batteries in that flashlight to make it work, because those batteries have special power in them. Now if I use that flashlight again and again, what happens to those batteries? They burn out. They don't have any power or charge left in them, do they?

I used to dump all those batteries out of that flashlight and go buy five more new batteries. Then I found this magic little gadget that really works. See this little black box. It's called a battery charger. If I open it up and we look inside, you'll see it has some springs and wire in it and some directions on what to do. If I took these batteries, which are old, out of my flashlight and put them in here, just like this (you can put four in at a time), then hook this up into an electrical outlet and close the box, the batteries would recharge. It takes them nine to twelve hours to recharge. Then a red light comes on, and my batteries are not dead anymore. I would be able to use them again.

There are times that our lives are like these batteries. Sometimes we need to get a charge. Sometimes we are really sad or unhappy. Maybe a best friend moved out of town, maybe your parents were upset with you, maybe you broke your favorite toy, and maybe you needed someone to come along and say, "That's okay. We'll find another friend." Or Mother says, "I'm not going to be too upset with you. Let's talk about this." But you get a charge. Somebody can do that for you.

Suppose you are really discouraged, and you have been standing on that free throw line, and you have been shooting those basketballs into that goal over and over. Then all of a sudden you get into the game, you try to shoot them, and they just don't go in. You say, "I'm no good at this." Somebody can come along, recharge us, get us all perked up, and we feel better. That has to happen in our lives sometimes, and you may wonder why I am talking to you about batteries and charges this morning.

I'm talking to you about batteries because of this poster and what it means. Have you seen these posters all over our church building? It seems that we are going to have a revival. What in the world is a revival? It is a series of special meetings, and we are going to have special meetings. It's special because we don't always come to church on Monday and Tuesday nights, do we? It's also special because we are going to have someone else come and talk to us. Our pastor preaches to us on Sunday morning, but we have a preacher coming to be our special revival pastor.

You may say, "OK, wait just a minute. We come to church enough. Why do we have to have these special meetings? Why do we have to come on special nights?" It all goes back to these batteries. Let's see if you can follow me. I told you that these batteries give the flashlight a special charge. Think about all the people who live around you who don't come to church and don't know that God loves them. We need to get them to church during these special meetings so they can get that special charge of light. When you get up on Sunday mornings, you know people who sleep, who don't come to church. We need to reach those people who don't know about God and His love and make sure they come to church. But you say, "Look at us, though. We're the people who are here every Sunday. We are in Sunday School and church. Why do we need to come to revival?" What did I say this little machine does? It recharges the batteries. All of us who come a lot to church may need to come to revival because maybe our batteries are getting a little bit dead or a little burned out. Maybe they need to be recharged. There is a very special verse in Isaiah that has to do with that. "But those who trust in the Lord for help will find their strength recharged" (Isaiah 40:31). So, if you trust the Lord, your strength and your energy to serve God will be recharged.

Let's pray. *Dear God, we do very much want to be a part of our revival. Help us to come so that we may charge our batteries or even recharge them if need be, so that our light shines to people all around us and so we can share that light and tell others that God loves them. Amen*

OBJECTS: Batteries/Poster/Flashlight

Let Jesus Rub Off on You

Some of you are doing projects at school with leaves, and you have probably put some leaves under paper and rubbed them to see if the print will come out.

This is a rubbing that was done from a piece of brass. In churches in England and in many abbeys, they allow you to make a brass rubbing. It works a little bit like this. (Of course, the brass rubbing would be done inside the church.) You would put the piece of brass under a sheet of paper, take your crayon and rub over it, and you would begin to see an imprint of what you have put under there.

The harder you would rub, the more the imprint would show. I just rubbed it briefly for you to see. This is a figure of a man, King Henry VIII, actually.

I have a rubbing of something here in our church. I want to see if you can figure out what it is. It's all rolled up here because it was big. It's a rubbing of our cornerstone. What is a cornerstone? It is usually a special piece of stone. It may be marble. This one was placed in the very corner of the foundation of our building when it was being built. It usually is put there when a lot of people are present, and there are many speeches made about the importance of the building. As you can see, it had things written on it. For instance, the name of this building and some special dates are on it.

Yesterday I came over here, taped this piece of paper over the cornerstone, took a crayon, and rubbed it across the cornerstone to get this rubbing. As I was doing that I had some thoughts. How is our church rubbing off on you? What do I mean by that? We talk about God here in this building. Do you talk about God when you leave the church? Jesus was very loving and kind, and He expects us to be that way. Do we wear our happy smiles when we are here in church, then leave them here and pick them back up next Sunday? We read the Bible a lot at church, don't we? Do you read your Bible outside of church? We are taught to be honest, to be caring, and to be helpful. We hear those things at church. Do we practice them when we go home? Do we think about that while we are at school?

At church we also do a lot of Christian hugging and handshaking. Are we afraid to do that outside in the world because we're afraid people will laugh at us? As I was rubbing, I wondered how much of what happens in our church is rubbing off on you. How are you letting it affect your life?

This is a Christian church, and we could not do it without God's help. Are you letting God help you through the week and letting the things that happen here rub off in your daily lives?

Let's pray. *Dear Father, help us by Your will and Your help through Jesus Christ to let things rub off on us. Amen.*

OBJECT: Rubbing

Smoothing the Rough Places

I have with me a brown piece of paper with some writing on it. If I turn it over, I imagine everyone knows what it is. It's sandpaper. I have some smaller pieces in my basket this morning, and I want you very quietly to pass them out to one another as I continue talking.

Sandpaper is made by using sand and gluing it to a piece of paper. It is made so that the sand doesn't come off very easily. It becomes a very valuable tool. As you get your piece, I want you to take it between your fingers and feel how rough it is. The neat thing about sandpaper and wood is that you can keep on and on, and the more you sand it, the smoother the wood becomes.

I want us to think about sandpaper and rough places. If this was going to be a bookend, I would have to work on it a long time because it still has some very rough places on it. Suppose you are sitting at the table, you put your elbows on the table while you are eating, you're doing your fork really funny, and probably your mom or dad try to tell you a better way to eat because they're trying to teach you table manners. They apply a little bit of what I call "human sandpaper."

Suppose you turn in a real sloppy paper at school, and the teacher knows you could do cursive a lot better than that. Some of you must have done that because you're smiling! The teacher hands it back to you and says, "I want you to do this paper over because I know you can do a better job." She's applying a little "human sandpaper." Suppose someone comes into your room and says, "Goodness, I would love the day I'd be able to walk from your door to your bed and not fall over." I know some youth up there are probably laughing at that one. Your parents are applying a little bit of "human sandpaper" to you. They are trying to help smooth out some of the rough places. You might have a friend at school or a person across the street whom you have ignored. You've decided that you don't like them as much as you once did. Maybe you should go over to them, use some "human sandpaper," and smooth out some rough places.

How do I know so much about rough places? I was your age one time, and I had a lot of rough places, too. Because of teachers, parents, friends, and some "human sandpaper," some of my rough places were smoothed out. But you know what? They are never all going to be smoothed out because they continue to be there as different kinds of rough places on adults.

There is a very special phrase in the Bible, Luke 3:5, that says, "And the rough places shall be made smooth." That phrase was talking about Jesus' coming and about the fact that He was going to help people like you and me know how to live a better life. I don't mean that He was going to come and teach us better manners or how to keep our room clean or to give us our papers back. He was going to teach us to lead a better life by being more loving and by being more caring and by teaching us how to give of ourselves to others. Let Jesus apply that smooth touch to you to help you smooth out some of the rough places that you have.

Let's pray. *Dear God, through Jesus Your Son, help make our rough places smooth. Amen.*

OBJECT: Sandpaper

Put on Your Blinders

What is that big word "temptation"? When I was thinking about temptation, I thought about my fourth grade school teacher, Mrs. MacFarland. I remember her telling us when we were doing our spelling or math, that some of us had "wandering eyes." They would sit there, then they'd lean back, then they might cross their arms, and they would look around on some other papers to see if they could find an answer to a question. I remember someone figured out a good way to find a math answer was to go sharpen your pencil. As you went to the pencil sharpener you could look around at someone's paper.

Mrs. MacFarland always knew what was going on in class. She would be at her desk, and we would think she was doing something else—grading a social studies paper or whatever—and all of a sudden, without calling a name or even looking up, she'd say, "You know, there are some of you in here that I might need to put some horse blinders on." And we thought, horse blinders! Here are some made out of paper, wire, and elastic. What happens when you put them on? You can't see out of the corners of your eyes. She was telling us that she was going to put horse blinders on us so we couldn't see out of the corners of our eyes, because we are all tempted everyday in different ways. We are tempted to cheat at school to get our papers done or to find the right answers, tempted sometimes to take things that don't belong to us. We might be tempted to do something that is mean or ugly to some of our friends. Jesus tried to tell His followers to say "no" to those temptations. This is what He said in Matthew 26:41, "Watch and pray that ye may not enter into temptation. The spirit indeed is willing, but the flesh is weak." That means that we may not want to do wrong, but we find ourselves saying "yes" to it every time we turn around. Jesus is telling us to watch and pray to God to make ourselves strong when temptation happens.

Let's pray. *Dear Father, all of us are tempted in different ways everyday. Help us to remember to talk to You and to be strong when temptation comes our way. Amen.*

OBJECT: Sign—Temptation

Controlling Your Tongue

What I'm talking about each one of us has. A tongue. Animals use their tongues in many different ways. A cat uses his tongue to lap up milk or water. A dog uses his tongue when he is panting to cool himself off. Frogs and anteaters use their tongues to flip out and pick up their food—bugs and insects they want to eat.

Each of you has a tongue, and our tongues are in there for many different reasons. Probably the main reason is to make sounds which then form our speaking. I want you to think about these words with me. Say this word: the. Your tongue went up to the front of your mouth when you said the word the. OK, let's look at this word: get. Your tongue started up toward the roof, and when you finally hit the t, it went all the way to the top.

Do you know that some kings used to have tongues cut out when there were people in their kingdom who were saying things the king didn't want to hear? This was his way of getting rid of it. Our tongue is dancing around in our mouth anytime we are talking, just like mine is going all sorts of ways while I am talking to you.

When you whistle, your tongue is going to roll a certain way so you are able to whistle. Did you know your tongue sometimes acts like a toothpick? When you eat some food and maybe a little gets caught in your teeth, your tongue goes in there and tries to pull it out like a toothpick. Sometimes your tongue might act like a policeman. Maybe you're eating a candy bar, you get a piece of paper in your mouth, and your tongue tries to push that piece of paper out as fast as it can.

Sometimes you use your tongue instead of words. Sometimes when you don't like something, you stick your tongue out at it. I also know that sometimes when your mother makes a really good pie or cake, you may lick your lips with your tongue to show her you really like it.

Your tongue is there for other reasons. It helps you taste. If you run your finger on your tongue, you feel little tiny buds. They are called taste buds because they look like tiny rosebuds. They have little cells in them that send something back up to the brain, and it tells you whether you like that food or not. Your tongue is also good for when you are sick. The doctor can look at your red tongue or yellow tongue, and he might figure out what is wrong with you. If it is purple, it might be because you ate some jellybeans, so you can't always go by the color of your tongue.

Once upon a time there was a lady who found out a juicy bit of gossip about one of her neighbors. She wanted to be sure everybody in her block knew. She went up and down the street saying, "Did you know . . .?" Pretty soon that gossip was all over town. Several weeks later the lady found out the gossip was not true, and it really hurt her because she realized what she had done to her neighbor. She went to a wise old man and said, "What am I going to do? I told this gossip about this woman, and it's not true. What can I do?" He said, "I'll tell you what I want you to do. Go to the market and buy a chicken. Get the butcher to kill the chicken. On the way home I want you to pull out the feathers from the chicken and leave a path." The lady said, "This is a wise old man, and this is something strange for me to do, but I'll do it anyway." As she went home, she pulled out the feathers, and left a path. She went back to the wise old man the next day and said, "I did as you said. Now what do I do?" And he said, "I want you to go back and pick up all the feathers you dropped." Well, you know what happens to feathers. They're very light, and the wind had come during the night, and the feathers were not there. She went back to the wise old man and said, "I went back for the feathers, but they were gone." And he said, "That's what happens when you spread gossip. It's easy to put the gossip out there, but it's hard to pull it back."

In the Book of James, James talks so much about gossip and about using our tongues. One of the things he said was that it is easier for us to tame a crocodile than it is for somebody to tame their tongue. That's really something, isn't it? This verse is very important, James 1:26, "Anyone who says he is a Christian but doesn't control his sharp tongue is just fooling himself and his religion isn't worth much."

Let's pray. *Dear Father, help us to use our tongues wisely. Help us to use them to say kind and truthful things and not use them in a harmful way. In Jesus' name we pray. Amen.*

OBJECT: Feathers

God's Trademark

Some of you will know this word. Trademark. It usually means that a company or someone in a company has invented a new product. The company begins to manufacture it and they sell it, but before they do that, they usually send the new product to the United States Patent Office, and it is registered. That means no other company should copy that product. So, if you see a trademark, it will have a little r with a circle around it, under the trademark, which means that the product is genuine. For instance, if I asked you what Coca-Cola is, I know everyone would shake their head. You may like New Wave or Diet. I happen to still like the Classic, but Coca-Cola is a registered trademark.

In fact, 99 percent of the people in a recent survey who were asked to identify this trademark knew it was Coca-Cola. Some other trademarks are Thermos, Kleenex, Xerox. When we first had Coca-Cola in the late 1800s, people shortened it and called it Coke. Today when we use the word Coke it could mean one thing to some people, but usually we mean a different-flavored soft drink. We are not necessarily saying Coca-Cola. Suppose I said, "I'm going to take something hot to work today (or something cold). Please bring me my Thermos." Really, only one company has the right to call this insulated jug a Thermos, and that would be the DuPont Company since this is a registered thermos, and it has the registered trademark under it.

If you have a cold and sneeze, you usually say, "Oh, I need a Kleenex." What you really need is a tissue because a Kleenex is a registered trademark of the Kimberly-Clark Company, but we have started calling almost all tissues Kleenexes.

Lots of times when I want to make a copy for you I say, "Oh, I've got to go to the copy machine. I want to Xerox this copy." I really should use the word Xerox only if I'm going to do it on a machine that is made by the Xerox Company and not a Minolta or a Toshiba. What has happened is that these trademark names — Coca-Cola, Kleenex, Thermos, Xerox, and many others — have become part of our everyday language, and they have lost some of their real distinctive value.

About 2,000 years ago in Antioch, the people who followed Christ were given the nickname Christian. In Acts 11:26 we read, "The disciples were first called Christians at Antioch." They were given a trademark. That trademark meant that they were followers of Christ. They tried to live like Christ, and they tried to follow His teachings.

What has happened to the word Christian through the years? We might say, "Oh, they are good Christians because they go to church on Sunday." "Oh, they were a good Christian because they didn't run that red light." "The members of that family are good Christians; they try to live a pretty good life." So we have sort of lost the distinctive value of our trademark of the word Christian. Christian to us should mean "followers of Christ," trying to live like Christ and trying to follow His teachings.

Let's pray. *Dear Father, we are so grateful to have the marvelous trademark of Christians, possible because of Your Son, the Christ. Amen.*

OBJECTS: Signs — Trademark/Thermos/Kleenex/Xerox/ Christian

Conscience: Our "Alarm Clock"

I brought my alarm clock with me. It plays seven different songs. This alarm clock intrudes on a lot of things. Does your alarm clock do that? Does it intrude on sleep? Well, this one does. It gets me up to do a lot of things I need to do. Perhaps you have to set your own alarm clock to get up just to catch the bus to go to school. Each of us has an alarm clock inside of us. My clock doesn't have one of those snazzy things where you hit it back down (snooze bar), go back to sleep for five more minutes, and then five minutes later it goes off, and you slap it down again. I see you laughing. You know, don't you? Sometimes that alarm inside us is doing exactly the same thing. We keep slapping that snooze bar back down. I'll give you an example. Suppose your mother had baked some brownies, you came through the kitchen just at the time she took the brownies out of the pan, and you said, "Oh, I've got to have one." She said, "Well, only one, because I have some ladies coming over this afternoon. We have a planning meeting, so you can have only one brownie." She gives you that brownie, then disappears to do some jobs someplace in the house. You're left in the kitchen with the plate of warm brownies, your hand goes up to those brownies, and you almost take one. That alarm clock inside of you is going off. "You really want to take that brownie? She'll never know you took it." But that alarm clock went off inside you and that's known as your conscience. The writer of the Book of Hebrews felt like the people thought he was not going to do things that were trustworthy. He was a little bit worried that people were suspicious of him, and so in his letter he wrote this, "Pray for us that we might have a clear conscience and that we might act honorably in all things" (Hebrews 13:18).

Many times we want to do something that maybe is not going to be honorable. Maybe we do something with our friends when we know we shouldn't. Maybe we were in the store and suddenly a pack of gum slid into our pocket. Our hand had to put it there.

Maybe we told a lie about something, but that alarm clock inside of us kept going off - our conscience. Did we listen to it or did we keep hitting that snooze bar and slapping it back out of our way? Let's try to be like the writer of Hebrews. Let's pray that we can act honorably and have a clear conscience.

Let's pray. *Dear Father, help us to listen to Your voice as it speaks to us in our hearts every day. Help us to have a clear conscience so we can be the kind of person You want us to be. In Jesus' name. Amen.*

OBJECT: Alarm Clock

"Wonderfully and Awesomely"

I want you to do some experiments with me. Suppose I said you had an itchy nose, told you to take your fingers and scratch your nose. Now I want you to scratch your nose, but I don't want you to bend your elbows. See if you can do it! No way to do it, is there? You can scratch your own nose only if you bend your elbow. Think of other things you couldn't do. You couldn't comb your own hair; feed yourself, or throw a ball. Aren't we glad God gave us elbows that bend?

Suppose that in front of you on the carpet is a pretty flower. Suppose I ask you to pick it up but not to bend your fingers. Some of you might be able to get it between your fingers, moving them sideways. You might be able to pluck it with your thumb a little bit, but it is hard to do if you can't bend your fingers, isn't it? You wouldn't be able to hold a pencil, you couldn't color, you couldn't tie your shoelaces.

Try this one. Look at me for fifteen seconds and don't blink your eyes. Make an effort not to blink. I blinked mine. Can you do it? It hurts. Your eyes start to become moist because our eyes are made to blink every five seconds, which means they blink twelve times a minute or 720 times an hour. Aren't we glad God gave us eyes that blink? Suppose I had to remember to blink my eyes as I'm talking to you (blink), and as I continue (blink) and as I keep going (blink). I wouldn't get anything else done but blink my eyes, would I? God gave us elbows that bend, fingers that bend, and eyes that blink - automatically.

King David felt that God has given us so many wonderful things. In Psalm 1:39, he said, "I will praise you, O God, for you have made me wonderfully and fearfully." If I use that word "fearfully," what do you usually think of? Something you're afraid of, don't you? It means something different in this verse. It's a word all of you know. Awesome. God made you and gave you a wonderful, awesome body. Suppose I ask you to repeat that after me. Before you do, I want you to put your tongue in the bottom of your mouth and don't move it. Repeat after me: God gave me . . . I can't hear you. Ok, we're not supposed to talk that way, are we? Our tongues are supposed to move.

I told you I didn't bring anything special with me this morning. I didn't need to because we are talking about all the wonderful parts that God put together in our bodies that work for us.

Let's pray. *Dear Father, You made the world in six days and in that time You made humans. On the seventh day You found time to rest. Help us to push aside all our noisy thoughts. Help us to rest from our work today, and help us to find time together in this place to rejoice in all the wonders of Your creation. You have brought us safely through another week. We ask our prayers come to You, our songs be lifted in joyous sounds, and our thoughts be pleasing to You. In Jesus' name we pray. Amen.*

OBJECTS: None needed

God's Love and Bears

Whether you want to admit it or not, at sometime or another, all of you had a teddy bear you hugged on and loved. Maybe you saw the koala bears at the zoo. I have a koala bear and other bears in here. This bear is dressed up for winter; he's a brown bear. A brown bear is known as a grizzly. I think it's really interesting that we hug and love on bears because they are some of the toughest creatures in nature, especially a grizzly bear. Grizzly bears grow to be as tall as ten feet and weigh as much as 1,800 pounds. Sometimes we hear that bears climb trees. The cubs of grizzlies climb trees, but the grizzly can't anymore because he's so heavy that as he tries to climb, he falls down.

The claws on that grizzly bear come out about four inches, and you can see why he can catch those salmon or why he could climb a tree. But a grizzly bear eats vegetables and meat, so you don't have to worry about what a grizzly bear is going to eat.

We don't think about bears running fast, but they can run as fast as forty miles an hour. They can run as fast as a horse can. A scientist might say that a grizzly doesn't know how to show love. But I think if animals know how to show love, a grizzly bear does. I'll give you some examples. A mother grizzly will do anything to protect her cubs. If she sees danger coming toward those cubs, she immediately does whatever it takes to protect them. There is a true story told of a trapper who set his bear trap. When he came back, he had caught a mother bear. The male bear was standing there hugging on the mother bear through the bear trap and crying. The trapper said he could no longer trap bears. Grizzlies take care of their young. Many times they take in adopted ones and begin to feed them. They teach their little ones how to swim, hunt, and hide. They teach them how to pick the bugs out of each other's scalp. The neat thing for us as human beings is that we have such wonderful examples of love, and it's so easy for us to see that love, the love of Jesus Christ. Jesus Christ came and lived. He died for us and then rose again. We can have that love of Jesus if we only believe. There is a very special verse for us in John 15:13, "Greater love hath no man than this, than a man lay down his life for his friends."

Let's pray. *Dear Father, we all do want to be loved, and we all do want to be hugged, and we thank You that it is so easy for us through Your Son, Jesus Christ. In His name we pray. Amen.*

OBJECTS: Teddy Bear/Brown Bear/Koala Bear/Another Bear

You Are Important!

All of you can see that I have a brick. One brick may not seem very important, but if a brick were not in my fireplace, my fireplace would be incomplete. If bricks were not in the wall on the side of my house, that wall might start sinking down. This one brick is most important. I also have one piece of a puzzle. To me that piece of a puzzle is going to be very important. I have this big puzzle spread out over a table. It's a hard puzzle. If I work that puzzle, and I'm missing one piece, that picture is not going to be complete, and I'm not going to be happy when I finish. This piece of puzzle to me is important.

I'm reading a book, and I can do this because it's my own book. If I took a page out of the middle of that book - one page - that means I'm going to lose some of the story, and I'm not going to know something that happened because I took a page out of it. That one page is important.

Each of you is important to God. Jesus told the story about a shepherd. The shepherd was standing up on a rise, and he was looking out after his sheep. He started counting them, and suddenly as he was counting, he found he only had ninety-nine sheep. He was supposed to have 100, so he went looking for that one sheep. Finally he found him, put him around his neck, and came back. The shepherd was so joyful, he began to have a celebration with his neighbors and the other shepherds because he had found that one sheep (Matthew 18:12).

If that one sheep is so precious to that shepherd, think how important each one of you is to God. This brick is important to my wall. This piece of puzzle is important to the whole puzzle. This page is important to my book. You are just as important to God. Do you have friends who need to know about God and His love? Those are special people you ought to think about bringing with you to church because they, too, need to know how important they are to God.

Let's pray. *Dear Father, thank You for letting each one of us be such an important person to You. You show us that by Your love. Amen.*

OBJECTS: Brick/One Piece of Puzzle/Book

The Lesson from "Fool's Gold"

Shake your head if you've ever panned for gold. Have any of you ever panned for gold in the Georgia Mountains in Dahlonogea? Possibly in the Tennessee or Colorado mountains? People have always tried to go where gold is, always hoping that they're going to "strike it rich." They'll set out with a pick, a shovel, a broom, a prospector pan, tweezers, a magnet, and they'll go where they can find gold. I did try my hand at it in the Little Creek Mining Company when I was there this summer. You need a pan, you need to go where there's a vein of gold, you put some of that dirt and clay in the pan, then you put water on it, and you take your hand and move that dirt and water to mix it up because the heavy things will go to the bottom. Then you begin to swirl it around in a circular motion and start dipping it back into the water. Well, that scared me to death. I thought if I had any gold, I was going to dip it all out in the water. But you keep trying, because the heavy part, which is the gold, will stay in the pan. This came out of the mine where I was. Look at the nuggets. Big nuggets. Shiny gold nuggets. You think I struck it rich? This is not real gold. This came out of the mine area where I was, but this is called iron or "fool's gold."

There have been many, many stories of people who found these big pieces of nuggets and thought they had found the real thing only to be told it was something of no value. The little piece of gold I found you won't even be able to see. See the bottom of this little pan. See that tiny little fleck. That's the real piece of gold. This is the fool's gold.

That's what happens in life many times. We're fooled by things. We don't know the truth, and we don't know the value. Think about the toy you just had to have and within two to three weeks' time, you no longer played with it because it was broken. It was not made well. You were fooled by the advertisement.

Think about when you wanted to eat a lot of ice cream and candy. You couldn't wait until your parents left, and you said, "I'm going to eat all the candy and ice cream I want." So you did, and you got sick. You were fooled, weren't you? Think about a time when you've had a friend, and you thought, This's going to be my very best friend. You've shared all these things with your friend only to find out that your friend is saying things behind your back, and you were fooled.

God doesn't want us to be fooled all the time. He wants us to learn what is valuable and what is true. God wants us to learn in our life what is true and what is of value. "All that glitters is not gold" (Shakespeare) and everything is not always true and of value.

Let's pray. *Dear Father, help us not to be fooled. Help us to look for what is true, real, and of lasting value. In Jesus' name. Amen.*

OBJECTS: Nuggets/Pan/Gold Fleck

What is This?

What is it? A hula hoop. You have played some games with these hula hoops. Let's try to see how many boys and girls could fit inside the hula hoop. Why did I bring it this morning? I brought it because it was the biggest thing I could think of that reminded me of a circle. When I think about God, I think of a circle. The Bible said that God is from everlasting to everlasting (Psalm 90:2). That's a pretty big word, "everlasting." But it means that God was here even before and that God will be here to the end. This circle reminds me of that because this circle has no beginning and it has no end. But as I also thought about putting it around each one of you, I thought of another part of what God does for each one of us and that's the fact that He is always circling each one of us. His love circles each one of us because He is always there for us. No, I'm not saying that God is this circle, but I'm asking you to look at this hula hoop and think about it as a circle, not as a hula hoop, but think of God from everlasting to everlasting, and the fact that His love encircles each one of us at all times.

Let's pray. *Dear Father, we thank You for being there for each one of us, the fact that there is no end to Your love which is always encircling us. Amen.*

OBJECT: Hula Hoop

Being a Lighthouse

Have you ever seen a lighthouse? Lighthouses, found on coastal areas, are built like towers. They're usually tall. The most important thing about a lighthouse is that at the very top of it, just as its name implies, there is a big, revolving light that goes around and around. Do you know what that light is doing? It's making sure that those ships will safely reach the harbor. It's sending out a beam of light so ships can see how to enter the harbor. I brought some other things that have a beam of light with me. I guess you know what this is. What is it? A flashlight. That's right. How does this flashlight work? What does it have in it? Batteries. This flashlight can be very bright. I'm going to take this one to camp with me. We use a flashlight to see where we are going if it's dark. I know some boys and girls use it under the covers when they're supposed to have their light out so they can continue to read, because I used to do that. It helps us find lost things or sometimes, if Daddy has to fix something, he needs to get that flashlight so he can see. This flashlight works on its own power source which is batteries. I have something else that gives off light. A light bulb. It has an electrical cord, and how does this work? It plugs into the outlet and it works, doesn't it? But it has to have its own power source. It has to plug in so that it works. This flashlight might look at this light bulb and say, "Hey, I've got you beat all over. I can go anyplace they want to take me." But the light bulb will have the last laugh. The reason is because we know that batteries die pretty soon, but as long as this light bulb is hooked into that power source, it gives us hundreds of hours of light. We're kind of like these lights. Jesus told us in Matthew 5:16, "Let your light so shine before men that they may see your good works and give glory to your Father who is in heaven." This flashlight has power unto itself. It's won't shine very long because it's unto itself. If we don't have enough power, if we try to do it ourselves, we won't shine very long. This light bulb we plug up can keep shining and shining. We are to plug up to Jesus so He can continue to give us light, so we can be a strong light shining for Him. We do that by the way we act, by the way we live, and by showing happiness and joy as Christians.

Let's pray. *Dear Father, help us to be beacons of light so we can share Your light with other people. In Jesus' name. Amen.*

OBJECTS: Flashlight/Light Bulb

Loving People Just the Way They Are

As the paper is coming around, I'd like you to take a piece because we're going to try an experiment. Follow my directions. Roll it up in a tube so you have about an inch in diameter. Put it up to your right eye, close your left eye, and continue to look through the tube. Now, what you want to do is bring your left hand up and put it next to the tube so your little finger is touching the tube. Be sure your left hand, the palm, is facing you. See if you can do that. Now, open both eyes and look. If our experiment worked right, what did you see? A hole in your left hand. That's an illusion, isn't it? Look at your hand now. There's no hole in your hand. If there was a hole, how did it heal so quickly? Maybe it didn't work for you right, but you can try it again when you get back home.

People are sometimes like that. We see only what we want to see. Think about someone you like a lot, and you may say, "He (or she) is really good-looking, or they're really attractive." But then you look at someone you don't like very much, you may say, "They're kind of ugly, or they don't act very nice." Sometimes we are looking at people just like we were looking through this tube. Our vision may not be exactly what it should be because those people may be putting on an act, and we are not seeing them in the same way. In Luke 15:20 we hear, "He got up and started back to his father. He was still a long way off when his father saw him. His heart was filled with pity and he ran and threw his arms around his son and kissed him." Most of you know the story of the Prodigal Son. You know that when the son came home, his father saw him, saw what he had been, but he ran to him, hugged him, and kissed him. He loved him just the way he was. That's the way your friends should be. They should love you just the way you are and see you just the way you are. What I want you to do as we look into the new year is to look at things as they should be. This was a visual illusion, but I want to be sure you have your vision on the things that are really important.

Let's pray. *Dear Father, we thank You that You can see us as we are and love us just the way we are. Amen.*

OBJECT: Paper

Memory and the Elephants

Suppose you went to the grocery store, and each day you had to bring back 600 to 1,000 pounds of groceries. I didn't say each week but each day. You would barely get enough food in the house for an elephant. They are not very practical pets, are they? Yet. they are most interesting animals - the largest beasts of the field. Elephants have many wonderful features. For instance, they have tusks that are really teeth, and many poachers (illegal hunters) for years have killed elephants for these tusks to use the ivory. These tusks can weigh as much as 300 pounds each. They are found on male and female elephants. Another interesting feature is the trunk. It's used for so many things: it's a picker because it picks the food and stuffs it into the mouth; it's a shovel; it's a plow; it lifts things; it's a backscratcher; it's a hose; and some people think it's a straw. Actually, water comes up in the trunk, and the elephant lifts that trunk around and puts the water into his mouth. So, the elephant's trunk is used in many, many ways.

The ears are interesting in the way they stand out to catch sounds. Many people say that the ears of the elephant are in the shape of the map of Africa (but there are also Asian elephants with smaller ears). Look at these big feet. They are padded, and the elephant can slip up on you, and you won't even hear it. Elephants prefer to be in the wild, but you have probably seen them in the zoo. You have seen them trained and performing in the circus. It takes twenty-two months for a baby elephant to develop and be born, but an elephant can live to be sixty to seventy years old. Elephants are creatures of habit. They may travel hundreds of miles each year, but they come back over some trails over and over. In Africa many of the highways were built on paths that were once old elephant trails.

There is one thing about the elephant that is not true. Everybody says that the elephant has a super memory. Elephants don't have any better memory than any other animal. It really doesn't have a better memory than most of us. How many times have you said, "I forgot my lunch," "I forgot my homework," "I forgot to give mother the message that someone called for her"? Many times our minds aren't any better than the elephant's. There is one thing we need to repeat over and over so we don't forget, and that is how much God has given us. Sometimes we want so many things we forget how much we already have.

I think God gave us minds that are better than the elephant's, so we can remember the good things our Creator gave us. In Psalm 103:2 we read, "Bless the Lord, O my soul, and forget not all his benefits."

Let's pray. *Dear Father, help us not to forget all You have done for us. Help us be thankful for each and every benefit. Amen.*

OBJECT: Elephant Pictures

Keeping Notes

We're going to pretend that this scene takes place in a family when they get home from church. This was an unusual Sunday morning because mother got up, fixed roast beef, potatoes, carrots, and green beans so when they got home from church there would be something yummy to eat. This family was at our church this morning. We'll call them the Martins. They had two children, Tom, who's ten years old; and John, who's six years old. When they got home from church, they sat down and were having a really good lunch, and all of a sudden John looked over and in this high, shrill voice said, "Tom, you have green beans under your chair. Look under your chair."

You know how little brothers are, don't you? Tom's mother looked under the chair, and said, "Tom, you're ten years old. You're old enough not to spill green beans on the carpet. We're going to smash them all over our carpet. You should know better than this." Tom was a little bit embarrassed. He was also a little bit angry at his brother for saying anything. John was so proud. Mother then looked under John's chair. She saw potatoes, carrots, and even some gravy from the roast beef, along with green beans, and she said, "John, you shouldn't have been saying anything about Tom. You've got enough food under your chair to feed the whole family." So Dad said to Tom, "On the way home from church today you were asking me about the sermon. The pastor talked about the log in the eye and the speck of sawdust. He read from Matthew 7. Daddy said, "This is exactly what our pastor was talking about." John was so busy pointing out Tom's faults and something he'd done with the green beans that he forgot to look under his own chair. I have another illustration of that. I have two notepads with me. Most of us have pads we keep notes on. I have to write things down so I don't forget. If I'm going to the grocery, I make a list. I imagine everyone of you has a notepad by your telephone so you can write down messages. Well, here's one that is a big legal-size pad and has a bunch of pages. This one is a little pad that doesn't have many pages in it. Suppose I'm keeping a list of all the things everybody does to me I don't like. I'm going to keep it in this big pad. So and so angrily stared at me today. Or I spoke to her in the hall, and she didn't speak back to me. Boy, my pad gets thick with of all the things I write down that other people do I don't like. But when I think about it, maybe there's some things I do that aren't so good. I have trouble writing something down. That's why this pad's so little, because it's hard for me to realize that I have faults, too, and that I ought to be writing my things down. This again is what we're talking about in Matthew 7. We're so quick to find faults with other people that many times we forget that our pad should be just like this. I think what Jesus wants us to remember is to look for the positive things and to major on those instead of always looking for the faults in one another.

Let's pray. *Dear Father, help us not to be so busy looking at problems/faults other people have, that we forget to notice our own. Help us to major on those things which are positive and to build good memories. In Jesus' name. Amen.*

OBJECTS: Two Pads

The Holy Spirit's Power

Let's think about the Holy Spirit. We can't see Him, and we don't know what He looks like. Why not? Let's see how the Bible says the Holy Spirit came. Jesus had been raised from the dead for about fifty days. His disciples were seated around a room in Jerusalem. They felt discouraged, helpless, and sad. Jesus had told them to go out and tell other people about Him, and they didn't even know how to start. Suddenly as they were in that room, something like a great wind blew, something like fire came and sat on each one of those disciples. They felt happy, and they had the power of God through the Holy Spirit in them. Suddenly, they were able to speak many different languages so they could then go and tell people everywhere about Jesus (see Acts 2).

Is the Holy Spirit still in the world today? Does God still use the Spirit's power to teach, strengthen, help, and guide us? Yes. His power can change our lives.

We are going to do an experiment today. This is one you might want to try when you get home, but I want it to represent something. Here is some vinegar, and here is some baking soda. These two things separate are not doing much, are they? I'm going to put this vinegar into this jar. I want this vinegar to stand for each of us. As I add this baking soda, notice what is going to happen. This soda represents the power of the Holy Spirit coming into our lives. Pretty neat reaction, isn't it? Two ingredients that by themselves didn't do anything, but when put together become something very powerful. I did this because I think this is how the Holy Spirit must have changed the lives of those disciples. When two things can come together, it can make a powerful difference. We need to let the Holy Spirit work in our lives and make that difference in the world.

Let's pray. *Dear Father, thank You for the power of the Holy Spirit. Help us to know how to use that power to accomplish much good in Your name. Amen.*

OBJECTS: Vinegar/Baking Soda

Raisins: Little, Ugly, but Good!

I brought a treat with me this morning. If you'll pass this bag around, you may take one of the smaller bags out of the larger one. As you look at what is in the bag, you are going to see something your grandmothers and your mothers are going to be baking in the next few days. You are going to be smelling raisin and mincemeat pies as we prepare for Thanksgiving.

Look at those little raisins. They're brown, shriveled up, tiny, and not much of anything, but they're good for you. Where do raisins come from? Grapes. We know that we put the grapes out in the sun, and they shrivel up. Grapes come from God. The raisins are such tiny, good little things. We are supposed to thank God for everything. Do you ever stop and say, "God is great, God is good, let us thank Him for the raisins"? That sounds silly, but we are supposed to thank Him for the little things. There is plenty around us we should be thankful for. The sun is not such a little thing, but we ought to thank God for it. What about the clouds that bring rain? What about the grass that animals need to eat which holds the dirt together? We have lights in our church so we can see. God didn't make the lights, but He gave man the ability to make them. We have pews to sit in so we don't have to stand up for an hour.

That would be tough, wouldn't it? Look at your clothing. You have buttons, zippers, velcro. These help you get in and out of your clothes. All of these wonderful things we have—man made these things but God was directing. I think you get my point. "In every thing give thanks." That's what the Bible says in Ephesians 5:20.

I didn't forget your raisins. I know you're going to take the only food in the sanctuary back to your pews. When you go back there I know you are going to open and eat them. But I want you, before you eat them, to think of something to thank God for. As you pop a raisin into your mouth, say to yourself, "Thank you, God, for _____." Because, "in everything give thanks." Not just for the big things in life, but for the little things.

Let's pray. *Dear Father, we are so grateful for everything You have given us. Help us to be thankful for the good, little things, as well as the big things. Amen.*

OBJECT: Bags of Raisins

We're Not Rocks

Can you guess what's in my basket? Rocks? That's exactly what is in here. How did you know that? Good ears? One of them is painted, but that doesn't make it any more special. One of them is just a flat rock. These rocks are just going to sit right here in my hand. They don't breathe, they don't move, they don't laugh. They don't do anything, do they? Suppose these rocks were to talk! I wonder what they would say. "I don't want to go back into that basket, I want to stay out so I can have some air." "Don't you hit against me." "Don't you push me." I don't really think that's what they would say. I think if they could talk, they'd say things like, "Praise the Lord" or "Jesus is King." Why do you think these rocks would say that?

There's a story in Luke 19 about Jesus riding into the city on a donkey. People were shouting all kinds of things really loud.

"Blessed be the King who cometh in the name of the Lord." Other people were yelling, "Peace in Heaven" - others hollering, "Glory in the highest." There were some people who were standing around by the side, and they liked everything to be prim and proper. They didn't like people shouting and making all that noise. They said to Jesus, "Tell your disciples not to do that." Jesus answered, "I tell you that if these disciples are quiet, the stones would cry out." Did He really mean that those rocks were going to start talking? I think probably He was saying to us that we have a wonderful God. He is so good to us. He sent His Son Jesus just for us. We think about His love and how much we love Him, but He doesn't want us to stop shouting and singing His praises. We shouldn't be shy and afraid to sing His praises, to pray to Him, and to tell everyone of His love.

Let's pray. *Dear Father, help us not to be like those rocks, but help us to continue to sing, to pray, and to praise Your name. Amen.*

OBJECTS: Rocks

Thanks for Our Eyes

Most animals can do things with their eyes that people can't do. For instance, if they're stalking prey, their left eye can look at a tree while their right one can turn around and look at a dangerous bobcat. Our eyes basically focus on the same thing at the same time. To show you that, let's perform this experiment. Look at this stick with me, close your eyes, now open just your left eye and look at this stick. Now open both eyes and look at the stick. It turned in a different position, didn't it? It stayed in one place when you opened both eyes, but when you closed your left eye, it was in one place and when you closed your right eye, it was in another place. You can continue to do it, but it will continue to change positions because we need two eyes to find the exact location and position of this stick.

God didn't want to leave us all alone here. He wanted to be sure we could see things from left to right, and He gave us a neck so we can look really fast from one side to the other. An owl can turn his head almost all the way around and look right behind itself. None of us can do that, but an owl's eyes can see really almost out of the back of its head.

A lot of people are color-blind. You may hear people say, "He must be color-blind. Why did he wear those clothes together? That looks awful." One out of every twelve men really is color-blind. That means they really can't see colors very clearly. Some of them can't see anything but grays, blacks, and whites. We are really lucky when we can see all the beautiful colors of God's creation. Look around at each other's eyes. Some of you have blue eyes, some have green, and some have brown. Blue and green eyes are more sensitive than brown eyes, but God gave us eyes with which to see His beautiful world. There are so many other things He has promised us that we are going to be able to see. We don't know if it will be in this life or when we have eternal life. First Corinthians 2:9 says, "No man has ever seen, no man has ever heard, no man has ever imagined what wonderful things God has ready for those who love the Lord." Many more wonderful things we are going to see with our eyes.

Let's pray. *Dear Father, we thank You that we can see. We can see Your beautiful world all around us. We are so thankful we are going to be able to see more things than we can imagine. Amen.*

OBJECT: Stick

Don't Strut Like a Peacock

The most beautiful and showy bird, I think, in all the world is the peacock. Maybe you've picked up a peacock feather. A peacock is the male pea fowl. Many times his train of feathers grows to be five to six feet long. This is not really the tail; this is just an extension of the feathers. Underneath these feathers, there are these tiny little stiff quills that push up the feathers so the peacock can be really showy. The kind that are the most common are the Indian peacocks. They're usually purplish, blue, or bluish green. We know about these eyes, don't we, surrounded by copper and bronze? But the female pea hen is not very pretty. Do you know what she looks like? She's kind of brown, and she has a little bit of a white tip on her. If you ever see a peacock pull out its feathers, you'll know it's the male because he's the one that has the most beautiful ones. Peacocks have been around for a long time. In fact, there are some Bible verses that have to do with peacocks. This one specifically says "peacocks" in the time of King Solomon. In 2 Chronicles 9:21, it says, "Every three years the ships came. They brought gold, silver, ivory, apes, and peacocks." But we also know that the Greeks and Romans thought the peacocks were sacred because they saw these eyes and weren't sure what the eyes were in the peacocks. Its feathers are kind of sacred to them, and they thought maybe a peacock was something they should worship. Peacocks used to be in large mansions and castles. They would use them as decorations in their yard, and a lot of people used to eat peacock meat. I think boys and girls sometimes are like peacocks.

You don't have to be around a peacock long if you're in the zoo to know that they're very noisy. They've got a loud cry like "help, help," and its very loud. They like to fight each other, and boys and girls can be that way. Sometimes, we think, oh boy, we've got the right kind of clothes, and we're good looking. We've got the right labels on our clothes and everybody should like us. It doesn't matter if we're selfish or disagreeable like these peacocks who are so showy. The Bible says that God looks on the inside. We find that in 2 Samuel 16:7 that "man looks on the outside but God looks on the inside." We don't want to just be like these peacocks, all showy and beautiful, but we want to have that inner beauty that only God can give.

Let's pray. *Dear Father, we do want to be attractive on the outside, but help us to realize how important it is that we're also beautiful on the inside, in our thoughts and our behavior each day. In Jesus' name. Amen.*

OBJECT: Peacock Feathers

Part II

Special Days

Scripture for Part II
(page numbers are in **boldface**)

Old Testament
1 Samuel 16:7, **90**
2 Kings 3:16-28, **88**
Job 37:14, **106**
Psalm 24:1, **103**
Proverbs 10:25, **104**
Isaiah 9:2 and 6, **78**
Isaiah 47:8, **110**
Malachi 3:10, **112**

New Testament
Matthew 2:10, **80**
Matthew 4:19, **95-96**
Matthew 5:9ff, **88**
Matthew 21:9, **94**
Matthew 28, **98**
Matthew 28:19-20, **86-87**
Luke 17, **113 and 115**
Luke 19:1-10, **91**
Luke 21, **84-85**
John 1:9, **80**
John 3:16, **91**
John 8:12, **77**
John 15:12, **90**
John 15:13, **107**
John 21, **95**
2 Corinthians 9:7, **111**
Ephesians 5:20, **114**
Colossians 2:14, **97**
1 Thessalonians 5:17, **92**

The Meaning of Advent

This is a special season for Christians to observe. Maybe you've heard this word, Advent. The word means, Christ coming, the fact that Jesus came as God's Son. It also means that Christ will come again. We celebrate Advent the first four Sundays before Christmas Day.

Some people use an Advent wreath. I want to tell you just a little bit about the wreath. First of all, around the bottom, it's made out of a round straw circle. The circle means that there is no beginning and no end. God always loves us; there's no beginning and there's no end to His love. Do you see all the greenery around it? In the wintertime all the leaves fall off most of the trees. There's something that's still green outside, and that's the evergreen tree. That's where it gets its name, which means that God loves us all the time, and that life continues to go on.

How many candles do you see? Five. There are four of them around the outside. What colors do you see? Pink, purple, and white. The purple candles stand for royalty. Kings and queens wear purple. Christ is our King. The pink candle stands for joy. We were so happy when Christ was born. But look at that white candle in the center. It's the Christ candle. It stands for Jesus, for His birth, and we light that special candle on Christmas Eve to show that Christ has come, since white stands for purity. As we light that candle, we remember that Jesus said, "I am the light of the world" (John 8:12). If you have ever gone down a long tunnel, it's dark. But you hope that when you get to the end of that tunnel, there's going to be light. That's sort of how the Jews felt. They felt like they were in a dark tunnel for hundreds and hundreds of years. They had been promised that Jesus was coming. They kept thinking, when is He going to come? When is it going to be light? So light that first candle as a candle of promise or as a candle of hope.

There was a little girl in the supermarket and tears were streaming down her face. She was standing by one of those horses (you put a quarter in, and you get on it and ride). She said, "But, Mother, you promised, you promised me." The mother said, "Be still, I don't have any money. You're not going to ride that horse." Well, she was crying, wasn't she? Sometimes our friends and parents break promises, don't they? They can't always keep them, but God never breaks a promise. There are many promises He made around the Christmas story. Prophets who were His men told us that Christ was coming. He promised Mary that she would be the mother of Jesus. The angels came to the shepherds and promised that there was a Savior born in a stable. The Jews had to wait many years in the country of Israel for God to come, but they waited, knowing that God would keep that promise. Some of them said, "It's been hundreds of years. Do you think God will really do that?" Some were making fun of the promise. Yet, other people said, "Yes, God always gives us hope through His promises." Isaiah, who was a prophet, told us this in the Book of Isaiah, a long time before Jesus was born.

> The people that walked in darkness have seen a great light:
> they have lived in a land of shadows, but now light is shining on them.
> A child is born to us, a Son is given to us:
> he will be our ruler, he will be called Wonderful, Counselor, The mighty God, eternal Father, Prince of peace
> (Isaiah 9:2, 6).

Let us pray. *Father, sometimes we have to wait. We have to wait our turn in line. We have to wait to grow up to become adults. We have to wait a long time for Christmas to come. The Jews had to wait for their promised Savior. Mary had to wait to have her baby Jesus, but somehow in waiting we can look at the candle we've lit this morning, the candle of hope, and we can sort of hear You saying, "wait, it's going to be worth it." Thank You for Your promise. Thank You for hope. Amen.*

OBJECTS: Wreath/Candles

Jesus: The Real Star

If I asked you what a star is, if I hadn't passed something out, you might think of your favorite movie star, and I think you would tell me the star of "Home Alone I" or "II," wouldn't you? Or you might think of your favorite singing star

Stars are used in decorations all over our church and in our homes. If you look at our tree, I even see a star at the top of our tree. I want us to talk about stars. I've given each one of you a star, too, and I want you to look at it as we think about stars. First of all, when can we see stars? At nighttime. Only at nighttime. If the moon is out, we don't see stars. It has to be a clear, dark night. Stars twinkle just as these stars are twinkling. Planets don't, but stars do. How do we see a star? We have to look, and we have to look which direction? Up. We have to look up to see a star. There have been people who have studied stars for years and years, and they've even found pictures in the stars, haven't they? We know about the Big and Little Dippers, and about a bear (Ursa Major and Minor), and about the Milky Way. How do we get to see this star? We see this star because light has reflected into that star for thousands of years. We don't actually see the star. We see the light that is reflected. They found a new star a few years back, but they say it's going to be thousands of years before man will be able to see it with the naked eye. Therefore, none of us are going to see that star are we?

I want to talk about a different kind of star. The star of Bethlehem - the star of Bethlehem was a very special star that God must have planned for years and years. He knew it was going to be over the manger and was going to lead many people to the baby

Jesus. So the star of Bethlehem carried a message . . . a message and other people to the manger. But you know we can use the star in another way because we can call Jesus "The Star of Bethlehem." Jesus was God's star, sent to each one of us, to show how much He loved us. As you put this star on your tree this Christmas I hope you will think about the star of Bethlehem carrying a message of great light showing people the way and also think about Jesus, our Savior who brings light into each of our lives. Matthew 2:10, "And when they saw the star they rejoiced with great joy." John 1:9, "And the true light that enlightens every man was come into the world."

Let's pray. *Dear Father, a star is born. That star is Jesus, Your Son, our Savior. We thank You for Him. In His name we pray. Amen.*

OBJECT: Stars

Francis and the Manger Scene

Francis was such a lively boy. He was full of energy and curiosity. If there was ever a crowd of children, Francis was always the leader. He lived in a hillside town called Assisi which is in Italy. His father had all kinds of money, so anything Francis wanted or needed, he always had. When Francis was a youth, he became terribly sick. His family was afraid he was going to die. During that time, Francis drew really close to God.

He would look at wheat and think of bread. He would look at clouds and think of rain. He would look at trees and think of shade and fruit. He decided that he wanted to spend his life helping poor, hungry, homeless people. He gave up all his rich robes and clothing, put on a patched garment with a rope around his waist for a belt. He went to tell his father he no longer wanted the money or the riches. People called him, "Caso, Caso" (crazy man, crazy man). He wanted to help poor people, and everywhere he went people began to follow him. He loved nature. There are legends that say if a little worm got in front of him, he would move it out of his way so he wouldn't step on it. One day there were all these birds in a tree and some people found Francis preaching to those birds, saying to them, "Now, you birds, you praise God because He has given you wings and freedom." During that period of his life he wrote a poem which many of you sing because it has been set to music, "All creatures of our God and King, lift up your voice and with us sing, 'Alleluia.'"

I want to share something about Francis when he was an older man in the year 1223. It was Christmas time. Francis was coming home one night very late with a friend. He looked out over the hillside, and he saw shepherds with sheep. It really made him think about that first Christmas when the baby Jesus was born. Francis was a pastor and teacher. He wanted to share that with the people in the village. He went out to a farmer and asked, "May I use your stable? Will you build me a manger? Can we bring live animals? Can we have a real Mary and Joseph?" So on Christmas Eve the people in the village took their candles and lanterns and walked from all over the mountainside to see the manger scene. Francis is credited with having the first creche or manger scene.

Most of you probably have a manger scene in your home. It may be a manger scene made out of porcelain, plastic, wood, or straw. But this one is very special to me.

Do you ever take the figures in your manger scene and move them around during the Christmas season? Do you ever stop and think what really happened and how it felt? Do you think, "Glory to God in the highest and on earth peace . . ."? Jesus came bringing us God's message, God's gift: "I love you."

Let's pray. *Dear Father, we thank You for the gift of love through Your Son, a free gift for each one of us. Amen.*

OBJECT: Manger Scene

Don't Forget the Christ Child

Only a few days before Christmas, Jonathan was going through the house carrying his brown paper bag, because he had put everything in there for a party - Christmas napkins, cups, microwave popcorn, hot chocolate mix, and candles. He was so excited. He thought to himself, Everybody is going to really love my idea. I'm going to go to Mom first because I know how much she loves a party. I know she's going to be excited with all this stuff I have in my sack.

So he went into the kitchen where his mom was baking, and he said, "Mom, I have this neat idea." And she said, "Jonathan, not right now. I've got to bake these cookies, and I'm trying a new recipe. Here, you taste one and take one to your daddy and go talk to him." So Jonathan went to find his dad and give him a cookie. He found his dad in the living room, and he had all the lights tangled up. His dad said, "Jonathan, why do we wait until the last minute to get this Christmas tree all together? These lights are always tangled. Please help me get them unwound so we can put them on the tree." Jonathan said, "Ok, I'll help. But Dad, I have this really neat idea." "Not now, son, I've got to put the lights on the tree if you want to decorate it today."

Well, Jonathan helped his dad for awhile and pulled the lights apart. Then he thought, "I'll go upstairs to my brother's room because I know my brother will think this is a really neat idea." So he did, and there was Scott, his brother. Scott was busy working at his desk. Scott growled, "What do you want, little Shrimp?" That really made Jonathan mad because he didn't like being called a shrimp. Scott said, "I'm busy making a present for Dad. This is going to be a really neat pencil holder for his desk at work. Just get lost. I don't have time for your dumb games."

So Jonathan took his little bag, went back downstairs, and sat in front of the fire. Unhappily, he said, "I have this neat idea, but nobody seems to have time for me." The wind was blowing, and suddenly the lights went out in the house. He could hear Scott stumbling down the steps. He could hear his mother coming from the kitchen calling, "Boys, are you ok?" He could hear his dad in the living room, asking, "Does anybody know where any candles are in the house? We've got to have some candles and get some things done." Jonathan said, "Well, Dad, that's kind of what I've been trying to tell you. I wanted to tell you about these candles." They all sat down in front of the fireplace, and Jonathan said, "I had this really neat idea. I've got four candles, like the four of us, and I thought we could each light one and tell why we like the person we are seated beside. And I've got all these other things, too, and I thought we could tell Christmas stories as a family." Everybody got quiet for a minute. Dad looked at Jonathan and said, "Jonathan, you know something. You're right. It's eight days until Christmas, but we've been so busy doing everything else that we forgot to take time for each other as a family and also to remember the Christ Child.

Let's pray. *Dear Father, help us in our preparations to know that we need to take time for our families - for each other - and to bring the Christ Child into our family time. Amen.*

OBJECT: Candles

Helping Foreign Missions

What are foreign missions? They are any kind of missions we do outside the United States. How can you as preschoolers and children help in foreign missions? How can you be a part of this week? There is a song called, "Hark, the Voice of Jesus Calling." The second verse is divided into two parts, and I want to talk about those parts this morning to show you how you can help. The first part says, "If you cannot cross the ocean, And the heathen lands explore," (heathen lands means places where people don't know about God), "You can find the heathen nearer, You can help them at your door."

There was a young girl named Mary Slessor, who was from a very poor family. Mary lived in Dundee, Scotland. When Mary was a youth, she had to go to work in a factory. She hated being in that factory from sunup until sundown, because Mary had a dream. Her dream was to be a missionary in Africa like David Livingstone. Mary thought, I'm going to have to work in this factory all my life. But coming home at night Mary would read her Bible, and she would pray to God that someday He would send her to Africa to be a missionary.

One day as she was walking home, reading her Bible, all of a sudden this whole gang of children just bumped into her and nearly knocked her down. She was about to fuss at them for bumping into her when she suddenly really began to see those children. Their faces were filthy, and they were very hungry. She looked at the streets where they were playing and saw how dirty those streets were. Mary said, "No wonder God's not sent me to Africa yet. I haven't learned how to help people at my own door." So she tried to be friendly to those children. She wanted to be their friend, and she started a Sunday School class for them. Some of those children later became preachers and teachers in their own churches, but God was getting Mary ready to go to Africa. Mary did become a missionary, and she did some courageous things which women had not done until that time. She crossed the ocean.

We are probably not going to cross the ocean and be missionaries. So how can we help? We know we can pray for the missionaries. That's what this week is all about. We can pray for their work there.

The second part of this stanza says, "If you cannot give your thousands, you can give the widow's mite; What you truly give for Jesus will be precious in His sight." I want us to think about the story in Luke 21. Jesus was sitting in the synagogue in Jerusalem. He was watching people as they gave their offerings. As people would give their offerings back then, they would say out loud how much they were putting in the offering collection area. One very rich man came up, and he nearly shouted at the top of his lungs so everyone would hear how much he was putting in. There had been some big gifts. Then a very poor lady came in and dropped her money in. I imagine she looked around and hoped nobody would hear what she had to say aloud. She said that she was putting in two mites. Jesus heard and then He made a very startling remark. He said, "She has given more than all the rest of you."

I want to show you what a mite looked like. It was a very small coin. It's this little one over here on the end. See how tiny it is? It was usually made out of copper or bronze, and she gave two mites. Do you know how much that was worth? One-half of one penny. Each mite was worth one-fourth of one penny. What do you think Jesus was saying? She gave what? All she had. When you are giving your offering to Lottie Moon, I don't want you to be ashamed of what you've put in it. We can't give thousands, but we can do a little bit better than the widow's mite. Whatever you give, I want you to give it gladly and thankfully, knowing that you can be a part of foreign missions.

Let's pray. *Dear Father, we confess that sometimes we are very selfish and therefore we are very stingy in what we want to give You. Help us to give what we can and what we are able. In Jesus' name we pray. Amen.*

OBJECT: Coin (mite)

Missions: Japan

I want to talk to you a little bit about Japan. Japan is a country smaller than the state of California. That makes it a fairly small country, doesn't it? It is made up of 3,000 islands. People live mostly on four of the largest islands. Who knows the capital city of Japan? Tokyo. People speak what language in Japan? Japanese.

In Japan it is said that no matter where you live, you can stand and see either the water or the mountains.

In Japan they do a lot of things a little bit differently from us. The only thing I brought to show you this morning is chopsticks, which are called the "hashi." They use this to eat their rice at breakfast, lunch, and supper.

I want to tell you a little bit about our mission work there. We have had missionaries in Japan for over 100 years. The land in Japan is very expensive. Can you imagine 122,000,000 people living in something less than the size of California? They can't build big churches like we have here. They don't have brick churches and big parking lots. You will find tiny little churches back in crowded streets. Missionaries have had to find ways to get people involved in church that we might not do here. In Japan it is important for schooling to come first in a child's life. Boys and girls start studying very, very hard from the first day they go to school because they have to take tests to pass to get into high school and college, and they want to go to the best high schools and colleges. Baptists have started a high school for girls and a high school for boys. Because we have these high schools, we can witness and talk to these boys and girls about Jesus. We also have friendship houses in Japan—places where people can come and learn to speak English, learn to cook, learn to do arts and crafts. Then we have our Baptist hospital there. Within recent years, a number of people learned about Jesus and were won to Him because of our work in that hospital.

It is amazing what things cost. Some places are very cheap. In Tanzania you can buy cereal for one week for fifty cents. In Japan you can buy a cantaloupe, but it costs you $18! We are supporting our missionaries all over the world and in 168 countries. We are doing that because in Matthew we are taught, "Go ye therefore and teach all nations, baptizing them in the name of the Father, the Son, and the Holy Spirit." I heard about four children who were playing one afternoon, and they decided to act out this part of the Scripture. They put on costumes of the different countries. One of the children said, "I'll play the Father." Another said, "I'll play the Son." Another said, "I'll play the Holy Spirit." The fourth child said, "Well, who do I get to play?" They said, "There is somebody named 'Amen' at the last part. You can be Amen." Let us go on "teaching them to observe all things whatsoever I have commanded you, and lo, I am with you always" (Matthew 28:19-20).

A little girl was telling her mother and father about what happened in Sunday School, and she said, "Mother and Dad, you always tell me to listen to what's going on, and you tell me to try to practice it and put it into my life. I was really disappointed because my teacher was talking about the Great Commission, 'Go ye . . . therefore . . . and teach all nations.' After she finished talking about it we all just sat there." We don't want to just sit here. We want to do something about that verse, and that's why we are putting emphasis on our foreign missions this week.

Let's pray. *Father, we hope that we really believe that verse when it says, "Go ye therefore and teach." Help us not to just sit here but to be an active part of foreign missions. Amen.*

OBJECTS: Fan/Chopsticks

Don't Foul in Life

I've heard a lot about basketball recently. I briefly thought about throwing this to one of you and letting you show me how to dribble, but I was afraid we might lose it down here. You know how to dribble, don't you? You drop the ball, let it bounce, then push it back to the floor. Most of you know the rules of the game and how to play basketball. I think we know how to do that pretty well. But sometimes we don't follow the rules exactly right. Suppose I got up and started dribbling with both hands? What would you call that? Double dribble. You would say I broke the rules; you're not supposed to do it that way. Suppose I happen to be fortunate enough to play in a game, and I walk over under the basket and put it in? What would you call on me then? I walked with the ball, didn't I? Sometimes we don't like that to happen in a basketball game, and we get very angry. Who is there to help us? God is there. Who else? The referee. He usually has a black-and-white shirt on with a whistle in his mouth. He's usually running up and down the floor, trying to keep up with the team and finding out what happens.

Sometimes we foul and don't mean to; sometimes we step out of bounds and don't mean to. When that referee blows his whistle at us, it upsets us, doesn't it? I have seen players get into huge arguments, and if the players get into arguments, usually the coaches start getting into arguments on the sidelines. Then people who are watching start getting into arguments. They accuse the referee of not being fair to the team, that he's giving them bad calls, that he's not being neutral.

There have been arguments for as long as we can remember. Remember Cain and Abel? Miriam and Aaron who were mad at Moses? Joseph's brothers who were mad at Joseph? Remember King Solomon? Two women came to him and were arguing about a baby. He simply said, "Give me a sword and let's divide this baby in half." The real mother spoke up and said, "Oh, no, I would never let you kill a baby" (2 Kings 3:16-28). The Bible says in the Beatitudes (Matthew 5:9ff.) "Blessed are the peacemakers, for they will be called the children of God." How do you handle arguments? Is it really simple for you to walk away or do you get in there and fight because you think you need to take sides? Are you going to be blessed because you are going to be a peacemaker and try to help settle things with kind words and by staying out of it?

Let's pray. *Dear Father, sometimes it is hard to walk away from an argument, but we ask You to help each one of us be a peacemaker, for we want to be blessed and children of Yours. Amen.*

OBJECT: Basketball

"Honest Abe" and Pearls

These pearls could be worth $15, $500, or as much as $5,000. Unless you are an expert, you don't know how much these pearls cost just by looking at them. You are probably wondering what kind of pearls these are. You can't tell by the outward appearance.

There are three different kinds of pearls—natural pearls, cultured pearls, and artificial pearls. A natural pearl is made when an oyster attaches itself to something in the ocean and a grain of sand gets inside the oyster. That oyster will try to get that piece of sand out. It will run as much as twenty-five gallons of water through its little body in a day to try to get that sand out. Sand is bothering the oyster, so it builds layers of pearl around that sand, and after a long time, you get a gorgeous natural pearl. If this necklace is a natural pearl necklace, it is worth $5,000.

Man has learned how to make pearls, so we can get "cultured" pearls. What man does is take these oysters in oyster farms, open them, and put sand in them. The oyster does the same thing. It builds around the sand. If this necklace is a cultured pearl necklace, it is worth $500. Or it could be an artificial necklace, and that means that glass beads are made in a factory and then painted to look like pearls.

Pearls can be white, pink, green, or gray. The rarest pearls are black pearls. They are hard to find and are very expensive.

Do you remember the fairy tale, "Mirror, mirror on the wall, who's the fairest one of all"? That is not a very good question, because we are looking on the outside instead of the inside. Most of you will know who this person is when I hold the picture up because his birthday is this month. When he was running for president, the people said, "How old Abe looks! He never even combs his hair." After he was elected president, he had an official picture made, and they said, "Oh, that looks just like you, but you've got to do something about that picture. There is something that's not good in it." And Mr. Lincoln asked, "What's wrong with it? It looks just like me." "Well, that's the problem. It shows all of your warts." And Mr. Lincoln said, "People elected me, warts and all, so I think what is important is not how I look but what is inside of me."

In the Old Testament when people are described, we have them telling us more about how they looked. For instance, you know that Samson had long hair. You know that David had beautiful eyes and that he was handsome. Think about the disciples in the New Testament. We know what they did, what they ate (sometimes), and where they went. But do we know what any of the disciples looked like? We don't really know what Jesus looked like, if He was tall or short, thin or fat, what size his nose was, what size his feet or hands were, because what is important is not how a person looks, but what is on the inside. A Bible verse says, "Man looks on the outward appearance, but God looks on the heart" (1 Samuel 16:7). It is not important whether we are pretty, ugly, tall, short, fat, thin, rich, poor, white, red, brown-skinned, or black-skinned. What is important is what is on the inside. The value is what is on the inside. I want you to think about Abraham Lincoln. It's not how he looked, but what he did and what was on the inside. I want you to think about Jesus, who said, "Love one another as I have loved you" (John 15:12).

Let's pray. *Dear Father, help us to remember that the most important thing in looking at our friends and people around us is what is on the inside. In Jesus' name we pray. Amen.*

OBJECTS: Pearls/Picture of Abraham Lincoln

Hearts Aglow

Most of you have a New Testament by now, and I want us to talk a little bit about this book, The Bible. Sometimes people talk about it favorably, and sometimes they talk about it unfavorably. It's a book that has influenced more lives than any other book in the world. In fact, it was the first textbook boys and girls used when they went to school. It's been on the best-seller list. It's been translated into over 1,000 different languages. If you will look at the very front of your Bible, there is a verse that most of you are very familiar with. The verse is John 3:16. You will find that it's translated in seventeen different languages. "For God so loved the world, that he gave us His Son."

We talked about God sending us His Son at Christmas time, the birth of baby Jesus. This week we've been talking about Jesus as a man and His last week with us on earth. As we think of Jesus, let's think of the way He taught us to love. When I cut out this heart, I ended up with four other hearts. Jesus taught us to love God with all our heart, soul, and mind. He taught us to love our neighbor as ourself. He taught us to love our mother and father. He taught us to love one another. Jesus loved many people. He loved the children. He asked the children to come to Him when He was very tired and when the disciples wanted to send the children away. Remember? Jesus also loved His friends very much. Remember the story of Zacchaeus and the sycamore tree? Jesus taught us that we need to love people. People are more important than possessions. But look at the last part of that verse. It says, "If we but believe, we can have life with him forever" (Luke 19:1-10). I've been cutting as I've been sitting here, because I wanted to finish cutting what this verse is all about. God so loved each one of us that He sent His Son to die on the cross for us. God's love is shown to us through His Son, Jesus.

Let's pray. *Dear Father, thank You so much for Your Son Jesus. He loved with a heart of love. Amen.*

OBJECTS: Bible/Paper Hearts

The Cross and the Pretzel

Lent is the period before Easter, during Holy Week, during Easter, and then the period after Easter (still the Easter season). During this season many of you may have eaten some special foods. Some people may have had hot cross buns. They are like cinnamon rolls and have an icing cross on top of them. These snacks used to be served only during the Easter season. This is the pretzel I have in my hand.

Many, many years ago, a monk, who was pastor of a church in Italy, was having trouble getting boys and girls to say their prayers. He decided to make a little treat for them which was what he called "a little biscuit." If you'll look at a pretzel, you'll see how they're crossed over, and it looks like hands crossed in prayer. He would give these pretzels to the boys and girls when they would learn their prayers. Then travelers took them over the Alps, salted and glazed them, and they finally came to the United States. We know that the biggest pretzel state is Pennsylvania. He gave them to the children to remind them and to reward them for saying their prayers. At one time they would be passed out only to poor people. Some countries, like Austria, put them on palm branches for Palm Sunday. It's because it reminds us of the reverence in which we hold this season.

Thinking about prayer, it's such a privilege that we can talk to God at any time and place. Many of us have been praying a whole lot during the Easter season. Right before Jesus left, He prayed for Himself, His disciples, all the people who were believers, and non-believers. He was trying to tell us that we can pray any time, any place. In 1 Thessalonians 5:17, we find a verse that says, "Pray continually," not just at crises and not just at the Easter season, but to pray at all times.

Let's pray. *Dear Father, we thank You for the Easter season. We thank You for Your son, Jesus. We thank You that we can talk to You at all times and that You hear us. Amen.*

OBJECT: Pretzels

The Amazing Palm Tree

I want to talk to you about palm trees. Many of you have been to Florida, and you have seen the palm trees. Those palm trees are very much like the ones in Jesus' time. I want us to think about the palm trees. First of all, they grow very straight. I think that says something to us boys and girls, because they want to grow straight. They don't want to have a lot of crooks and curves in their character.

Palm trees are tall, aren't they? Some grow to be eighty feet tall, but most of them are about forty to fifty feet tall. There's a hymn that goes, "I'm pressing on the upward way, new heights I'm gaining everyday." Do you know what that means? You need to keep reaching for the very top and trying to get there to be the very best you can be.

When winds are blowing the palm trees, you can see them bending over and swaying, and you think, How in the world are those trees staying up? The winds are very heavy, particularly in Florida where they have a lot of hurricanes, but because those palm trees have sent roots way down into the ground, they are able to withstand all that wind, even though all the leaves and fruit are at the top of the tree. That's what you need to be doing as boys and girls in church—putting down roots. You are doing that as you come to Sunday School, study your Bible, and learn about Jesus. These trees are always green. It's not too hot, too cold, too wet, or too dry for a palm tree to keep going on about its business. I can't always say that about church business, can you? Some Sundays it might be too cold or too wet.

There are as many as 360 products that can come from a palm tree. In fact, it has often been said that people who live in a very hot part of the world (Arabs and Egyptians) could live off a palm tree. First of all, you have the fruits: dates and coconuts that can feed millions of people. Then, you have these palm branches. They take these and weave them into baskets, mats, and couches. Next, they use the timber that comes out of the trunk of the tree. They use its fiber to make robes and rigging for boats. They also use the sap from the tree to drink. There are so many uses of a palm tree. Just think: if God can take a palm tree and get that many uses out of it, what could He do for your lives as you try to grow straight and tall, as you try to put down your roots, as you try always to be green, and then, as you let God use you in the way He would want.

These palm branches were used by the Jewish people as pictures or symbols of peace and victory. We have just enacted Palm Sunday. Jesus was coming into Jerusalem, and He sent His disciples to find him a colt. He said He wanted a colt which had not been ridden. If you have ever watched a rodeo or if you have been to a horse farm, you know that a colt has to be broken in, and it takes a long time. It takes a period of many weeks before you finally put the saddle on. The last thing that gets on is a person.

Jesus got on this colt that had never been ridden before, and the colt must have sensed His gentle manner as He was coming into town in this parade, and people began to shout, "Hosanna! Blessed is he who comes in the name of the Lord" (Matthew 21:9). They put their garments and palm branches out in front of Him, because Jesus was showing us that He was coming in peace. This was a great sign of victory for us as Christians.

Let's pray. *Dear Father, help us to remember the palm trees in our own lives, that we will grow straight and tall with special roots and foundations in our church. Thank You so much for letting us be a part of Your special parade, Palm Sunday. Amen.*

OBJECT: Palm Branch

The Sign of the Fish

The night after Jesus' resurrection He went to an upper room where His disciples were meeting together. They were frightened when He came into the room, and showed them His hands and feet. He said, "Peace be unto you." I guess they probably didn't really believe it was Jesus until He sat down and ate with them. Then almost a week later, which is about the time we are at now, Peter and six of the disciples went out fishing. They stayed in that fishing boat all night and threw their nets over the side time and time again. But they didn't catch anything

As it began to dawn, they saw someone standing on the beach, and this person said, "Have you caught any fish?" They said, "No, we haven't." He said, "Well, cast your net out on the right side of the boat." They thought, Who in the world is this man telling us to cast our net on the right side? We've been throwing that net back and forth all night long. But they did as He said, and so many fish came into the net that they were not able to pull it up into the boat. As they got closer to the shoreline, they saw that this person was Jesus. They didn't have to say, "Who are You?" They knew it was Jesus. He said, "Come on in and bring some of the fish you have caught. Let's have breakfast together." As they came in, they saw the fire, and they took breakfast with Jesus. He gave them the bread and the fish (John 21).

That's two times when Jesus appeared to His disciples where we also see fish in the story. In fact, in many of the New Testament stories about Jesus we find fish. Do you remember when He called the twelve disciples? He called seven of them who were fishermen. That's how they made their living. But more importantly, Jesus said to them, "Follow Me, and I will make you fishers of men."

We also know that Jesus told a lot of fish stories—not like some of the fish stories some of you tell—to emphasize God's love. In the Bible we find many different signs and symbols. Jonathan gave his belt to David as a sign of their friendship. God put a rainbow in the sky as a promise to us that never again would the whole earth be covered in a flood. You remember that one of the most special signs we have is the Star of Bethlehem which led shepherds to the nativity. Let's bring it up a little to modern days. Think about your parents and the rings on their fingers. The rings are a sign or a symbol of their marriage and love for each other. Many times when you are driving down the street, you see pink or blue bows on mailboxes or front doors. That's a sign or symbol that there is a new baby boy or girl born to that family.

The early Christians wanted a sign or symbol to let other people know that they were Christians. From everything I've said you're going to know what it was. What was it? Take one and pass them out. The sign was the fish. When the Christians first decided to take the fish as their symbol, they were afraid that people would harm them if they said they were Christians. So what would happen if two people were talking to each other? In the dirt or sand, one of them with their toe would make half of the sign of the fish. If the person they were talking with happened to be a Christian, what would they do? Make the other half of the fish sign. But later, as it was ok and they weren't afraid of being hurt, they began to wear the sign of the fish around their necks. They began to make it out of the olive wood and put it into some of their furniture which they made, because it was now a sign that was all right.

As you look at your fish, and as you take it with you to your seat, I hope you will look at it as a symbol of what we are — Christians — but more importantly, think of it as a picture of Jesus' love for us and what He said, "Come, and I will make you fishers of men" (Matthew 4:19). Your responsibility is to tell others about God's love and about His Son, Jesus.

Let's pray. *Dear Father, thank You for symbols that sometimes makes things easier to understand that are hard to explain with words. Thank You for the symbol that shows who we are and who You are. Thank You for the greatest gift of all, Your Son, Jesus. Amen.*

OBJECT: Fish Symbol

The Crown of Thorns

This Sunday is a great time to talk about hats because I knew some of you would have on hats this morning.

This is a rain hat that will protect me in the rain. This is a hat somebody might wear to play in the snow. There are hats we can look at and know a person's job by the hat they wear. If I hold this one up, what kind of job would you say they had? Fire chief. How about this one? Policeman. How about this one? Pilot. How about this one? Captain of a ship.

Jesus wore the most special hat of all. Because of the hat He wore for us, we have Easter Sunday. That very special head covering or hat He wore was the crown of thorns. For Christians, the symbol of Easter is the cross. If Christ had not worn this crown of thorns, we would not have the cross as our symbol of Easter. Jesus did die. He was dead for three days. He was restored to life because He was God's Son, and because of His sacrifice each of us can have eternal life. Many people wear crosses around their neck. We are reminded of Jesus and all that He accomplished when He was here on earth, but the cross also should give us the feeling of hope of everything we should still be doing through His love for each of us. In Colossians 2:14, we read, "He canceled all our debts out when he nailed them to the cross."

Let's pray. *Dear Father, thank You for this happy, happy day. Thank You for raising Your Son Jesus. We do want to walk with Him every day. In His name we pray. Amen.*

OBJECTS: Hats: Rain/Snow/Fireman/Policeman/Pilot/Captain

Jesus, the Caterpillar, and the Cocoon

I have a caterpillar and a cocoon. It attaches itself to a branch and begins to spin so the cocoon becomes like a small tomb. Several weeks later, that cocoon bursts open, and out comes a new creature—a beautiful butterfly. Something strange and wonderful happened on that first Easter Sunday, too. Jesus was laid in His tomb on Friday. It was a tomb much like a cave. A large stone was rolled in front of the opening. Early on Easter Sunday several women wanted to go to the tomb to anoint Jesus' body. They talked to each other and said, "How can we get inside? How can we roll away that large stone?" Suddenly there was a strong earthquake, and the stone was rolled away. An angel appeared and said, "Do not be afraid. Ye seek Jesus who was crucified. He is not here. He has risen. Go to Galilee and tell His disciples."

Well, you can imagine the women were somewhat afraid, but they were filled with joy. So they hurried on their way. As they were leaving, Jesus appeared to them. They fell at His feet and worshiped Him. He said, "Peace be with you." Something strange and something wonderful happened. Jesus was alive indeed. This is the story of the resurrection, as told in Matthew 28.

Let's pray. *Our risen Lord and Savior, we give You thanks, and we give You praise for the gift of new life. We know that we, too, someday will rise again. Help us to share this good news. Amen.*

OBJECTS: Caterpillar/Cocoon

Help Home Missions to Walk

Home missions is all about sharing the love of Christ with those people right where we live. In order to do that, we must be prepared. Today I have several ways to tell you about preparing yourself.

You have to have the right kind of shoes — this is very important. Construction workers sometimes have shoes with steel toes in them, so if they drop something on their foot it won't be broken into a million pieces. Logging people many times have hobnails and cleats on their boots. Some people wear a metal arch support in their shoes. Many of us pick out our shoes because we like the way they look rather than the way they feel. I know many women who, when they first step in their house, kick their shoes off. So, you must have the right kind of shoes.

There's a story about a farmer who was going to take his geese to market. He wanted to sell them and get a really good price, but he didn't have a truck to take them in. He knew those geese were going to have to walk to market. Geese have webbed feet, and those feet are good on the dirt and grass, and they're great for swimming, but they're not good for walking on coarse gravel. The farmer thought, What am I going to do? By the time I get them there, their feet are going to be all swollen and bloody, I'm not going to be able to sell them. He thought for a few days, and he cleaned out two pens in his barn. In one of the pens he put some warm tar and drove all those geese into where the tar was. You know what happened? The tar stuck to the bottom of their webbed feet, and then one by one, he lifted them over into the next pen where he had put sand. The sand stuck to the bottom of their tarred feet. Those geese now had wonderful walking shoes! When the farmer got to market, he sold them for a good price. When I say you have to have the right kind of shoes, I mean you have to be willing to go. You may say, "Ok, I have the right kind of shoes, but what in the world am I going to say?" My suggestion to you is this—take a blank piece of paper. At the top write this phrase, "How I Know God Loves Me." As you make that list, you're going to realize that if God loves you in those ways, He also loves those people around you in the same way.

We've done the easy part. We've got the right kind of shoes, and we know what we're going to say. The hard part comes when we actually have to go and tell a friend about Jesus. In our neighborhood there is no way we could talk to everyone. In fact, in the United States there are at least 167,000,000 people who don't know about Christ. These people are red, yellow, black, white, rich, poor, young, old, single, married, urban, and rural. There is no way we can reach them. That's why as Southern Baptists we have and support over 4,000 home missionaries across our land. We support them by prayer, and by giving. You'll have your chance next Sunday. I know you want to be a part in telling, giving, and praying that those people might believe. Let's pray.

*Dear Father, thank You for the many, many ways in which You
love each one of us. Help us to be willing to tell those around us,
to be willing to give help to those we can't reach, and to pray for
all those people who don't know about You so they might believe.
In Jesus' name. Amen.*

OBJECT: Picture of a Goose

The Trinity and the Shamrock

A person told me one time that a shamrock was a rock? I think
most of you are aware that it is a plant, and particularly connect
the shamrock to Ireland. Ireland is a long way from us. People in
Ireland are familiar with the shamrock because it is their official
plant. Everything you see about Ireland almost always has a
shamrock on it.

On March 17 each year we celebrate St. Patrick's Day. Many
of you are going to wear a shamrock, possibly on your sweatshirt,
blouse, or jacket. People will wear them on their suits, blouses, or
shirts. On St. Patrick's Day it is Irish to wear green. We also know
that sometimes the Chicago River is dyed green. In New York City
down 5th Avenue, a wide line is painted green. If you look at any
ads in the paper for grocery or department stores, you are going to
see little shamrocks in them. You might even eat a green piece of
bread or a green bagel, because on St. Patrick's Day everything
comes out green.

A legend is a story about long ago, and it may or may not be
true. There is a legend that says that St. Patrick planted shamrocks
in Ireland. He planted them in Ireland because they were
three-leafed, and he had a special reason for planting those
shamrocks. I am going to pass around some shamrocks to you. As
you take one as I continue to talk, I want you to look at the
shamrock. It is three-leafed, but the neat thing about the shamrock
is not only is it three-leafed, but each leaf looks like it has three

tiny little leaves in it. The word shamrock means "three-leafed." As the legend goes, St. Patrick came to Ireland. He wanted to live with the people, he wanted to teach the people about God, so they say he planted these shamrocks so he could talk to the people about the Trinity.

This is a big word. TRINITY. What does that have to do with the shamrock? We said that the shamrock had how many leaves? Three. Trinity stands for three. Trinity means three, and it means the three ways which we talk about God - God the Father, God the Son, and God the Holy Spirit. Look at your shamrock. Let's look at the first leaf on it. Let that stand for God the Father—a great parent who made and created the whole world. Let's look at the second leaf on it. Let that stand for God the Son, Jesus Christ. The fact that God loved us so much that He sent His Son, Jesus, whom we call Christ. Let's look at the third leaf. Let that stand for God the Holy Spirit. Jesus' followers really experienced what that meant when Jesus died on the cross. They knew that God was close to them, as near as He had ever been through the Holy Spirit.

As you wear your shamrock on St. Patrick's Day, I hope you will look at it in a different way. Think of it as a plant with three leaves, but also think of it as the Trinity: God the Father, God the Son, and God the Holy Spirit - God who creates, God who loves, and God who inspires.

Let's pray. *Dear God, thank You for letting us see You and know You in these three very special persons. Amen.*

OBJECT: Shamrock

Caring for God's Earth

Many of you probably do Earth Day projects and experiments in school. Sometimes trying to do something about saving our earth can be overwhelming, and we think there's not anything we can do. But there are many things you can do as children. I want us to look at some of those things.

We can recycle. A lot of you do this. I see bags in your homes by the back door. You can recycle toys by giving them to other children. A lot of you save aluminum cans. As Americans, we use 65 billion aluminum cans every year. If we average that out per person, it means we are using an equivalent of 256 cans per person a year. That's a lot, isn't it? We can also recycle plastic. It's estimated that we use as much as sixty pounds of plastic in a year per person. Think about how light this plastic is and how much it would take to get sixty pounds. A lot of you don't even weigh sixty pounds. So we're talking about stuffing this plastic until we get that much. Cardboard is something we can recycle. We know we can recycle cardboard from cookies or crackers or whatever as long as the cardboard is gray on the back side. Many of you are into recycling.

There's something else we can do, and that's helping to keep our earth green. You say, "I'm green today - I'm sick." You're sick and don't go to school, but we want our earth to be green because it means it's healthy. We can reseed. We can plant seedlings and trees. This paper bag is something we see a lot at the grocery store, because we get our groceries in it. A tree that grows for fifteen years will make 700 paper bags, but you can go to the grocery store and count the paper bags given out, and in one hour's time, 700 bags will be given out. Yet it took one tree fifteen years to grow to make those paper bags.

We need to conserve water. Do you know that just by faucets dripping, most of us lose enough water to fill a whole swimming pool in a year? That's not talking about water that sometimes, when we turn it on, it's not cold enough to drink, and it's not hot enough to wash our hands or the dishes, so we just let it run.

We also need to watch pollution and try to conserve energy. Only one-tenth of the energy of a light bulb (when it's on) goes to actually put the light inside the bulb. The rest of it is the heat that surrounds the bulb.

There are things you as children can do to help Earth Day and our world. Psalm 24:1 says, "The earth is the Lord's and everything in it, the world and all who live in it." God made a wonderful world. He fit everything together. He put us in the world in charge of it, but He didn't want us to sit here and destroy His world. So remember, the earth is the Lord's.

Let's pray. *Dear Father, we thank You for Your creation and this world. We thank You that You created us to be in it. Help us to know how to use the world properly and not to ruin or destroy it. In Jesus' name. Amen.*

OBJECTS: Aluminum Cans/Plastic Bags/Cardboard/Paper Bags/Newspaper

Dandelions Are Really Dandy

If you look at this dandelion it looks rather innocent. It has pretty little green leaves, jagged and pointed. Do you know that we spend thousands of dollars each year trying to get these weeds out of our yards? Many of us work on them; we hack and cut them. One person told me they used to send their children out to dig up dandelions, and they would pay them a penny for every dandelion they dug up. We do battle with these "weeds," as we call them. This dandelion can grow just about any place. No matter how much we cut it back or dig it up, it is still going to grow.

We know dandelions get into our yards, don't we? How about downtown in the concrete? There can be the tiniest crack in that concrete, and what can happen? That little dandelion seed can put down roots and start growing, right there in the middle of downtown. Someone coming home from a lunch break could kick that yellow flower off or a truck could back up and smash it, and you would think the dandelion couldn't survive, but what happens? They just keep coming back. They're tough. No matter how much I get them up, they're going to multiply. I think maybe we ought to change our attitude about those dandelions and learn something from them.

We could wear them in our hair, couldn't we? They are flowers, aren't they? How many of you have taken bouquets of yellow dandelions to your mother or your father? My mother used to say the dandelion should be the national flower; so many little grubby hands have brought a dandelion bouquet into their parents. You were so proud of the flowers you found. Some people even eat these leaves as a green vegetable; some countries make beverages out of them; some make medicines from them. I want us to learn that the dandelion is tough. It comes back and stands firm. I think that for boys and girls, we need to learn how to stand firm. We are going to be neglected, abused, and trampled on. Think about those little dandelions in our yards and how they stand firm.

There is a special verse in Proverbs 10:25, "When the storm has swept by, the wicked are gone, but the righteous, honest people stand firm forever." Our faith in Jesus Christ helps us to stand firm.

Let's pray. *Dear Father, help us to look at that little weed we have in our yards which causes us so much trouble. Help us to remember how strong and firm it is and for us to be that way as Christians. Amen.*

OBJECT: Dandelion

Thanks to God for Plants

We have some visitors this morning. A lot of you are visiting your grandparents this spring, and we're glad. Have you been noticing all the signs of spring? All the growing plants? Did you see the beautiful daffodils in our front lawn of the church the past two or three Sundays? You might even have some blooming at your house.

This is something that's in bloom in my yard. It's a shrub called forsythia. Last year one of the Sunday School teachers had a bunch of these branches in a vase, and she was telling the boys and girls over and over that the name of this was forsythia. Finally, this one little girl said, standing up with her hands on her hips, "Mrs. Turner, I'm four years old, but I can count, and there are more than four sythias on that branch!" This is an azalea. Look how it is almost ready to pop open into bloom. I imagine you have some of these in your yards because Atlanta and Decatur have a lot of azaleas.

What surprises me the most are the trees. They just look absolutely dead without leaves on them, don't they? Then all of a sudden, now that it's spring, look what's happening. This branch I would have thought would have fallen off. It didn't even seem alive, and now look at all the leaves beginning to come out, and a sweet gum ball is beginning to appear. Jesus lived in Palestine. It's March in Palestine, and it's also springtime in Palestine. When Jesus was a boy and walking the streets (they were dirt, not like our paved streets), He would see many beautiful bushes and flowers blooming. Birds are flying back to Palestine just like birds are flying back to Decatur because they have been South for the winter.

Jesus had fruit from some plants He was able to eat. You have eaten most of these, but think in your mind what they look like and what they taste like. In Palestine at this season Jesus would be eating grapes, raisins, olives, apricots, and almonds. You have tasted those, haven't you? God gives us plants that are beautiful to enjoy, and He gives us fruit from plants to eat.

He gives us plants for another purpose. Look at this tree. This tree makes violins so you can play it. This tree helps to make shoe polish. It helps us to build houses; it's a home for birds and squirrels; it gives us oxygen to breathe; it helps make paper, pencils and books; and it also helped to make this poster.

But one thing we can't make that God gave us is a seed. God made each plant so it makes its own seed and can continue to grow.

There is a lovely verse in Job 37:14, and I want to read it to you. "Think about the wonderful things that God does."

Let's pray. *Thank You, God, for spring. Thank You for creating plants that we use and enjoy, and that are so beautiful for us to look at. Amen.*

OBJECTS: Forsythia / Azalea / Tree branch

Memorial Day

Boom, boom, boom! A 21-gun salute rings through the air. A band stands rigidly at attention, and a speaker's voice echoes over the microphone. Then, relatives, friends, and strangers start walking among the graves where their flowers have been placed, and flags are fluttering in the breeze. Then, in the distance we hear the sound of the lone trumpeter as he plays taps. That's something which will be repeated many times as we celebrate Memorial Day—a day in which we honor those who have served in our Army, Navy, Air Force, and Marines.

The idea for Memorial Day started in 1865 after the Civil War. Henry Wells of Waterloo, New York, said, "We need to remember those people who fought brother against brother and uncle against nephew." Is there anything more important than being alive? I think the history of our country and its wars shows us that there are things more important, and the Bible tells us that there are things more important than life itself. The history of our country and wars shows us that freedom is most important to us—something we have fought very hard to have. Truth is very important to us. There have been many struggles of truth over falsehood and peace over war. Peace is very important to us. It is strange to say that we have peace because we fought to get it. But the history of our country, through the Civil War, two World Wars, the Korean, and the Vietnam wars, shows us that freedom, truth, and peace are important to us.

Jesus himself showed us that there are things more important than life. In fact, He was willing to give His life that we might have these things—salvation, forgiveness of sins, and peace with God. In fact, in John 15:13 Jesus said, "Greater love hath no man than this, that a man lay down his life for his friends." Jesus did that for us. Soldiers in our armed forces have laid down their lives so we might have freedom, truth, and peace. Let's take a few minutes to think about those things that are really more important than life itself. Let us remember the people who have made those things possible.

Let's pray. *Dear Father, we do thank You for the freedom we enjoy as Americans. We thank You for the gift of Your Son, the Prince of Peace. Amen.*

OBJECTS: Military Medal/Insignia

The Trophy of the Cross

Ann gave her father a beautifully wrapped package, and on top of the package was a little plastic trophy. When a swimmer, track star, or basketball star receives a trophy, they've really earned it. They're proud of it, and they want to put it where people can see it. This was a plastic trophy which said, "To the World's Greatest Dad." Ann's father took that trophy and placed it on his bedside table so he would see it the first thing in the morning and the last thing in the evening. You may wonder what he did to earn that trophy. Well, if we asked Ann, I'm sure she could give us many reasons why she felt her father was the world's greatest dad. But the father said, "It's just an inspiration to me because I get up in the morning and go to bed at night, and I do want to be the world's greatest dad."

Trophies can be really expensive. Some of them cost hundreds of dollars, and some are inexpensive. This little plastic cup Ann gave her father probably cost less than a dollar, but it wasn't the value that was important - it was what it meant to both of them. We win all kinds of trophies. We like to get trophies like this loving cup. Many of us are members of clubs and organizations which give us a silver tray with our name engraved on it, and we are so proud of that - we may receive a wooden plaque we can hang in our office on the wall, or win medals or ribbons. In fact, this one was given to me by someone's parent last year when we started to camp. It says "The Boss." I don't know if it helped. Or we may get a diploma or a degree. You look at this and think, That's not worth very much; that's just a piece of paper. But think about the hours of work and study that went into getting that diploma.

I'm talking about trophies because as a Christian there is a trophy that means a lot to us, and it's a trophy that is portrayed well in our baptistry. If you'll look up there you'll see the cross. What did it cost? What does it cost? How do we earn that trophy? Well, it cost a man, Jesus, His life. Jesus died on the cross and lived His life for others. He lived His life so men and women, boys and girls might have a better way of life. As Christians we have the right to wear this trophy or carry it in our pockets. But we also need to be sure we have earned that trophy. Have we made our profession of faith in Jesus? Have we accepted Him?

There was a youth who was a swimmer and had earned so many medals and trophies that in his bedroom one whole wall had medals on it. He had about three shelves where he had all these special trophies. Nobody ever got to see them unless his parents took them into his bedroom. They were so proud of him. Every time someone came to the house, they would always say, "Please come and see our son's trophies." The boy had reached another point. He said, "Those are things I did in the past. What can I accomplish in the future?" He didn't want to rest on his laurels. Do you know what laurels means? A long time ago, in the Greek games (like the Olympics), they would give instead of a trophy, silver tray, or a diploma, a crown of laurel leaves which were woven together and put on your head. That crown usually withered and died, so when you came back to the event again, you had to earn a new crown. You had to re-earn your laurels. That's what we as Christians need to do. Not only do we need to earn our trophy (the cross), but we need to re-establish that relationship and keep growing as Christians.

Let's pray. *Dear Father, help us to have our trophy before us at all times so we can truly be a bearer of the cross that others will know we are Christians by the way we act and the way we live. Amen.*

OBJECTS: Plastic cup/Trophy/Loving Cup/Silver Tray/Wooden Plaque/Blue Ribbon/Diploma

Labor Day

There's always a lot of excitement at the airport. People are bustling around, they are excited, and some people flying for the first time have a little bit of fear. I like to watch people in the airport. I like to see who is waiting to pick up which people. Sometimes people bring flowers and sometimes they bring candy.

Those of you who have boarded a plane know there is someone there, usually a flight attendant or an airline official, who takes your ticket and boarding pass. Then you go onto the ramp and enter the airplane where you also have a flight attendant who helps you find your seat. Well, over the PA system, they began to announce, "Last call for Flight 246 leaving at Gate 5." The door closed. About that time, a man came with his suit bag and briefcase to Gate 5. He said, "I've got to get on that plane. That's my plane. You've closed the door, and it's leaving." He began to bang and wave his arms. He was really being obnoxious. So, the Delta person who was in charge, called the pilot and said, "We have someone who has arrived. Do you think this man can get on the plane?" The plane opened the door, and they let the man through the ramp, and he got on the plane. The plane started out to the runway, and suddenly the plane turned around and came back because the man should have gotten on Flight 347 which was boarding at Gate 7. Everybody who was at the airport started laughing because it was funny to them. It was full of a lot of bad characteristics, I think, for that man. He hadn't paid attention to the baggage porter who had told him which gate to go to. He had forgotten to be at the airport thirty minutes early. He didn't have any concern for other people, and he was being very crude. Another word I could use is that he was just plain careless.

Isaiah the prophet had something to say about that. He wrote, "Hear now this: thou dwellest carelessly that sayeth in thine heart, 'I am and none else beside me'" (Isaiah 47:8).

We are all careless at times. When you get something new and decide to put it together, you would think the first thing you read is the first direction. You don't read all the way through. You fathers, when you are putting things together (tricycles and all), you start with the first direction, don't you? You don't read all the way through because sometimes when you get to direction 7, it says you should have done this before this. Those of you, when you do your schoolwork, do you go back and check to be sure you did all your problems, or did you skip a row and not even notice? How many times have we had to go home because we weren't sure we turned the stove off? Or we might have left the iron plugged in. We all need to be very careful in our work and not be careless, and we particularly want to think about that on Labor Day.

Let's pray. *Dear Father, we are so grateful for our work, be it at home, at school, at church, or at a place of business. Help us to do our work as carefully as we can. Amen.*

OBJECTS: Airline Ticket/Boarding Pass

Stewardship: Giving to God

I have some pieces of paper with me. Checks. You've heard your parents talk about their paychecks, haven't you? They need them so they can pay for the house, for the electricity, for things at the grocery, and for your clothes. They must have money in the bank to cover these checks.

These checks are for different things. What does this one tell me it's for? Can you see it? $10. Let's see what the next check is for. You could get a new bicycle with this check. This one says it is good for a color tv for your own room. Getting even better, isn't it? But this one says $1,000,000. If I asked you to pick which one of these checks you would want, which one would you pick? $1,000,000? That's what I thought.

Everyone of us in here is already a millionaire. You're going to say, "Wait a minute. I didn't work one day or one hour to get money to be a millionaire, so how could I already be a millionaire?" It's so very simple I'm ashamed sometimes when I realize how much we already have and how rich we are, because of the things God has already given us. Most of us have two eyes that see. I wouldn't trade these eyes and give up seeing mountains, streams, flowers, insects, and sunrises, nor could I buy them for $1,000,000. You have two ears so you can hear the beautiful sounds of nature and music. Many people can't hear, yet they can't buy ears through which they could hear for $1,000,000.

You have taste. I wouldn't want to give up being able to taste peppermint or chocolate or vanilla milkshakes or hamburgers or strawberries. Some people cannot taste, and yet you cannot buy the sense of taste for $1,000,000. You have the sense of touch—you can touch and feel things that are good and things your hands know not to touch (hot stove), or when to put on mittens so your fingers won't freeze. All of these things God has given us. You have the sense of smell. I love to smell bread baking. Many of you like to smell coffee. There are so many wonderful smells. God has given us all these wonderful things that we could not even purchase for $1,000,000. He has given us so much, and yet it makes me wonder why we are not willing to give something back to Him. The Bible says that "God loves a cheerful giver" (2 Corinthians 9:7) and it also tells us we ought to "bring a tithe of our money" (Malachi 3:10). You know what that means. If you have a dollar, you are supposed to bring ten cents back to the church. You say, "Wait a minute. If I bring only ten cents on Sunday, that's not going to add up very fast." If everybody in here brings their tithe, that money begins to add up, which means we can do things in our church, in our neighborhood, in our state and around the world. When you get your allowance, think of saving some. Spend some for things you need. You have been a part of something great here this morning. You were in Sunday School. You were a part of the music ministry if you sang. Maybe you are active in missions. Why not be a part of being great by bringing God something back because He has given you so much?

Let's pray. *Dear Father, each one of us is very rich because you have given us so much. Help us in turn to learn how to use our money wisely and to give something back to You. Amen.*

OBJECT: Checks

Be Thankful

On a stormy night, September 6, 1860, Edward W. Spencer, a student at Garrett Bible Institute, was walking along the shore of Lake Michigan. He saw that the waves on the lake were starting to become rough, and he saw a tragedy happen. All of a sudden a big freighter carrying lumber hit the side of a steamboat named The Lady Elgin. Edward Spencer knew that ship was going to sink . . . 393 passengers were then thrown into the water. He thought, What can I do? I don't have time to get to the town closest by. They wouldn't have enough ships. The only thing he could think to do was to swim out and try to save as many people as he could. He went back and forth seventeen times and saved seventeen people. He never got over the tragedy of that night. He had to go to a hospital, and in a few years he was confined to a wheelchair. He became an invalid. He never could go back to college to finish his studies, because he kept thinking, Wasn't there something else I could have done?

A smart newspaper journalist was going through some files, and he came across the original file from Chicago. This guy had been compared to a national hero. The journalist thought, I wonder what's happened to this hero. Wouldn't it be great to follow up and see where he is? So he started trying to track down Edward Spencer and facts about his life. He went to interview him on his birthday, and said, "Please tell me the one thing that sticks out in your mind about that night. You were such a hero for seventeen people." And Edward Spencer said, "Not one of the seventeen thanked me for saving them!"

Gratitude. Thankfulness. We neglect them even now. We all know the story in the Bible of the ten lepers. We know that they came to Jesus full of their woes and asking to be healed. Jesus told them to go to the priest in the neighboring town. He said, "Show yourselves to the priests. They are the medical authorities to say whether or not you have been cleansed or not." These lepers had to turn around and leave Jesus. It had to be an act of faith because He did not heal them right there. As the lepers were walking away from Jesus, they looked down and saw their skin had been cleansed. Only one turned around, came back to Jesus, and shouting in a loud voice, praised Him, saying, "Thank you." The Bible says that this one person who came back was a Samaritan. That is really interesting because a Samaritan was a foreigner in that country and supposedly had not been educated as well. Yet he was the only one who gave a first-class thank-you to Jesus. Jesus, more out of sadness than anger, looked at this leper and asked, "Were there not ten of you cleansed? Where are the other nine?" (Luke 17).

Those two stories don't give us a very good response rate, do they? Zero out of seventeen thanked Edward Spencer. One out of ten thanked Jesus. Where were the other people then, and where are we now? As surely as we all sit here, we know that the fourth Thursday in November is Thanksgiving. You have been talking about Indians and Pilgrims in school. It is one day we set aside to really count our blessings and give thanks. We try not to grumble, and we try not to complain on that day, but there is something I wish we would do. I wish we would set aside a day in which we would say, "This is going to be the day we are going to grumble and complain," and then take 364 days to be happy and give thanks to God. In Ephesians 5:20, we find, "Always and for everything give thanks to our Lord Jesus."

Let's pray. *Dear Father, we have so many things to be thankful for. We have so many blessings we can't name them all. We can't count them all. Help us to be thankful always. Amen.*

OBJECT: Thanksgiving Display

The Pilgrims and Thanksgiving

We have a special holiday coming up this week, and some of us will be going to visit grandparents, and some of our grandparents will be coming here. Or we might be with aunts, uncles, and cousins because we do know it's Thanksgiving.

It was a very determined group of men, women, and children who got on the Mayflower to come to a new world. There were 102 Pilgrims, thirty who were officers, seamen, and captains, but by the time they got here (it took a total of three months), there were only ninety-nine people left. There were two babies born on the Mayflower—Oceanus Hopkins and Peregrine White. Most of the other children had names like John and Elizabeth, but those were two unusual names.

They got here in winter and it was cold. It was a very hard first winter. Many of the Pilgrims died during the winter, but most of the children survived. Their food got so low that they didn't have much to eat. At one point there is a record that Elder Brewster gave thanks for a cup of water and some clams he had. He gave thanks to God for the blessing of the sea and for the treasures he found in the sand. It was such a bad winter that their daily food allowance went down to five kernels of corn.

I have brought candy corn, and you must remember that these are bigger than kernels of corn. I didn't say five ears of corn, I said five kernels of corn! That's all the Pilgrims had to eat daily during that first hard winter, but they were blessed because they met an Indian named Sequanto, and he taught them how to plant the corn. Sequanto said the best time to plant was when the leaves on the oak tree were the size of a mouse's ear. That would be a tiny, tiny leaf, wouldn't it? He told them to hoe an area of land about six feet and to make a small hill - then take these seeds and put them into that hill, but also to plant fish in the hill. On the Mayflower there were two dogs that came over. You know what happened when they planted the corn? The dogs kept digging it up and eating the fish, so they had to tie the dogs up and guard the hills so nothing would happen to the corn. They were very fortunate because they had a really good crop. They harvested all of this Indian corn. It was different from our corn today. It was short and knobby, and it was in different colors. They roasted it and ate some of it, but much of it they made into cornmeal so they could have cornbread or cornmush. Then they used the husks and stuffed them to make mattresses. The girls also used the husks to make little dolls. So it had really been a wonderful first year for them because they had actually been able to raise their food. They stopped and gave thanks to God.

We now live in a land where most of us don't have to worry about food. None of you here are going to be hungry on Thanksgiving Day, and you don't have to worry about whether or not you are going to be in a nice, warm house. But think about those Pilgrims who made it through that first cold winter with only five kernels of corn a day to eat, and the fact they stopped and gave thanks to God.

In Luke 17 there is a story of the lepers. "Jesus was walking down the road between Samaria and Galilee and there were ten lepers who were afar off, and they cried to him, 'Master, help us.'

And Jesus, as they came toward Him, said, 'Go, and show yourselves to the priest.'" As the lepers started walking off, they looked down at their skin which had been diseased, and it was soft and healthy. Only one leper came back and thanked Jesus and knelt at His feet.

As you sit around your Thanksgiving table this year, I hope as a family you will give thanks to God and not forget and leave Him out. Don't be like those lepers who went away and forgot to thank Jesus!

Let's pray. *Father, help us to give thanks because You have given so much to us. You even gave us Your own Son, in whose name we pray. Amen.*

OBJECT: Candy Corn